A Devotional

TIDBITS OF WISDOM

A-Gem-A-Day

SANDRA E. JACKSON

Co-Author Beverly J. Renford

62 Days of Devotion

"As the hart panteth after the water brooks, so panteth my soul after thee, O God." (Psalm 42:1)

ACKNOWLEDGEMENTS

From: Sandra E. Jackson

I would be remiss not to acknowledge my village as I fully understand that it takes a village to support an individual in becoming all they could be in life.

My village is:

My oldest son Theodore Jr., you have been a consistent support to me by making sure I laugh uncontrollably. Your support rendered to the family will always be appreciated.

My second son Brandyn, your constructive criticism has forced me to push harder in every area. Your zest for life and your passion for singing and recording is remarkable.

My eldest daughter Brittany, your energy and passion towards life gives me insight into unconditional freedom. Your support for the family is well appreciated.

My third son Benjamin, your view of the world has enhanced my passion to travel the earth without apprehension. You have gifts and a promise to remain faithful to God and there is no limit.

My fourth son Solomon, your life change has given me extra faith to believe God is faithful and will not forsake His people. Your personality is remarkable, and you will be all God wants for you. Your gift shall make room for you.

My second daughter Diamond, your total life has been appreciated. You have that thing inside of you from God. As you assist me with my passion, just know I appreciate every minute you have lent. Fly!

My third daughter Victoria, your generous heart has been a true asset to the entire family. You have special gifts that I pray you take the time to hone into. Soar!

My fourth daughter Sandra, you have been gifted with precision and a love for life. I pray that God will guide every step and that your dreams come to fruition. Run!

My fifth daughter Schrene, you have been a burst of joy for the entire family. You are gifted with multiple tools. I pray you stay the course and live for God as it is His desire as well as mine. Go!

Lastly, to my Lord and Savior Jesus Christ. I breathe because of you. My life would have gone in a different direction had you not stepped in and guided, protected, and provided for my children and me. I am eternally grateful to you for life, health, and strength. You push me daily and for that alone I am grateful.

From: Beverly J. Renford

I honor my 9th grade English teacher, Mrs. Patricia VanKouwenberg, whom we addressed as Mrs. VanK. Due to our move to Penfield, New York, that summer, I was no longer a recipient of the Urban-Suburban initiative. In May of my 5th-grade year, the Rochester City School District had obtained parental permission for me to be enrolled into, one month before the school year ended.

Upon finalizing 8th grade, I had graduated in the sanctuary of St. Louis Church, in Pittsford, NY., and that summer, the Rumph family moved to Penfield. I attended Bay Trail Middle School. That fall, we were told that our teacher was in England and therefore, we would have a substitute English teacher until after the Christmas break.

I struggled with William Shakespeares' *"Macbeth," "A Midsummer Night's Dream", and* everything of that genre which was presented within those four months. The A*'s* which were my normal grade in English began to slip.

Returning from the break, a young, short in stature, overly curly-haired, jubilant female stood before the class in the Teaching Auditorium and introduced herself as our permanent teacher. We were expecting the teacher whom we had all heard would appear.

Her enthusiasm, and youthful skill opened my mind to understanding, and enjoying the classics in a way that I had never experienced previously. Mrs. VanK is the teacher who showed interest in an African-American, eager to learn, student who stood approximately a foot taller than her. She birthed into me creativity, and a flair for writing.

I honor my sister: Evangelist Sandra E. Jackson for a plethora of reasons.

I honor my Parents: the late Bishop Samuel I., and Elect Lady Sister Priscilla M. Rumph.

I honor My husband of 40 years: Elder Mark A. Renford.

I honor our eight offspring: Brooke, Bridgette, Rachel, Nicole, Benjamin, Courtney, Anastasia, and Markaysia.

I honor our seven grand-blessings: Shiloh & Sage, Brayden & Bryan, Preston, Penelope & Priya.

Most of all, I honor the God of Heaven, for his tireless, abundant mercies.

TABLE OF CONTENTS

FOREWORD

In 1917, there was an international slogan used to promote cereal that read, "Breakfast is the most important meal of the day." Like many natural aspects of life, this saying also applies to us as spiritual beings. As Christians, we understand that starting everyday by feasting on the Word of God is crucial. Thus, our devotional and communion time is an essential part of the day in which everyone should partake. The only way to develop a personal relationship with the Father is through consistently spending quality time. I am aware that it is easier said than done, but remember the goal is that we may know Him. The fellowship is about so much more than the things we suffer. The psalmist wrote, "Serving the Lord will pay off after a while." I say, "it pays off daily with new mercies, joy everlasting, peace in times of trouble, and benefits that have yet to unfold."

As a publisher, I get my fair share of manuscripts, but working on this book has been different. The presence of God hovered as the author and I went over changes for the project. It was as if God was putting His mark of approval on it. When God's been good to you, you can only contain your praise for so long, even when it is business. Both the author, Sandra E. Rumph-Jackson, and co-author, Beverly J. Renford, heard me mention not writing the foreword for this book until I was inspired. I said, "the book would be alright without having a foreword." I have learned to follow the direction of God, so when I wasn't inspired to write, I didn't. Then I found myself in a place, after a long day at work, where God would not let me rest. When inspiration comes, it's best to make time for it. Thus, I began writing this foreword. This book will help its readers. Deliverance will occur, chains will be broken, and someone will be set free from the torments in their mind.

Each day we receive twenty-four hours (1,440 minutes) to do the things that God has called us to do. How much of that time do we spend in His presence seeking direction and a deeper understanding of Him? This book's daily devotions range from one to ten minutes, with most of them being under four minutes. Of course, no book can ever take the place of reading your Bible, including this one. For those who struggle with prayer, consider this a conversation starter. Read each devotion for its respective day and pray accordingly.

Through reading God's word, we learn His heart towards us. We also see our mindset towards Him. We know what He thinks of us through His Word, but how do we feel about His word when it pushes us towards things contrary to the flesh and its lusts? Revival is only attainable through God. Saturating ourselves with His word revives us again and again. As you read this book, do not miss your opportunity to dig deeper by opening your Bible, worshipping, and praising God. As I said, these devotions are just conversation starters; the presence of God will meet you. Be that as it may, we all know that real blessings only come when you stretch out a little further. But do not stop at reading and reaching; start walking. Seek His face and not His hand.

Ebony Lynnel Harris
BE Publishing Co.

INTRODUCTION

In today's world, it is easier than ever to feel as if you are experiencing an influx of life's pressures. Many people are overwhelmed with life's circumstances to the point of despair. Shaking their heads, searching for answers that seem to be intangible. What I would like for you to know is: I've been exactly where you are. Following the end of my marriage, and even post-divorce, my whole world was topsy-turvy. I felt the sting of embarrassment and the heavy burden of failure. It was due to life's excruciating pain that I will never forget the day when God showed me that He still sees me. He extended His arms of compassion and restored me to a place of peace. He then left me with an assignment to catapult others from where they are now to a place of thriving in His perfect will. I am ecstatic to not only be able to encourage others verbally and vocally- but through the written word as well.

God awakened me early one winter morning and urged me to write this book. At first, I came up with: Estelle's Daily Devotions as the title. Next, it was Estelle's Tidbits of Wisdom. It was not until I completed the last word that it impressed upon me that the title had to be: Tidbits of Wisdom. God instructed me to seek whether my sister would join me in this exciting venture. I received a swift reply of acceptance. Upon asking her if she wanted to add to the title, she offered, "a gem a day." Hence the complete title of this book.

For many years, my sisters and I have prayed daily via phone call and have built a foundational relationship with our Creator. It is through that daily experience that we have learned His heartbeat. I would like to challenge you during your reading to chase after Christ as if it were the last thing left on your bucket list. As you read this book - along with your Bible - God will open your understanding to receive the spiritual insight, wisdom, and knowledge only found in Him. As God speaks, take notes. As He instructs, obey. He has all the answers and has given us everything that pertains to life and godliness. I hope that this book will assist in catapulting you to your next level in Him. Blessings galore on your new journey.

ALLOCATION I

DAY 1

PAY IT FORWARD

Reading time: 2 minutes

Devotional Scripture:

"I had fainted, Unless I had believed to see the goodness of the LORD in the land of the living." (Psalm 27:13)

Heart To Heart:

In life, we struggle with unbearable situations which may cause us to stumble, or to feel like life has dealt us a bad hand. That is when we have taken our eyes off of God and have put them on our situation. If we remain focused, steadfast, and unmovable we shall reach our goal. Jesus is the main source of our help and if we sincerely cry unto Him, He is willing and able to come to our rescue. His help is free. It comes without suffering and pain. It comes without regret. He leaves no residue.

The psalmist has requested the favor of the Lord. He realizes he needs the benefits of the Lord's divine protection so that, when all others have failed us and we have failed ourselves, it is vitally important to know that there is a God; a God who will keep us from utter destruction from the calamities that befall us repeatedly.

Fainting is not an option for you. Look closer and you will be able to see the God-vision that has been strategically canvassed for you.

We must encourage others as the word of God encourages us.

Food for thought:

It's refreshing to pay it forward.

DAY 2

WE HAVE DAILY BENEFITS

Reading time: 2 minutes

Devotional Scripture:

"Blessed be the Lord, who daily loadeth us with benefits, even the God of our salvation. Selah." (Psalm 68:19)

Heart To Heart:

Jesus Christ, through His life, death, burial, ascension, and resurrection has been given authority by God to grant to us His benefits daily. Because He suffered, bled, died, and rose again He is equipped with the tools to divinely provide His people with loads of blessings continuously. Open your mind and clear your brainwaves so you too can receive the benefits from up above each day. He has no prejudices. Christ came to a rebellious world. He didn't come to condemn it, but that the world through Him and His suffering might be saved. He is available to as many as will accept Him. 1 Corinthians 10:13 states, "there hath no temptation taken you, but such as is common to man: but God is faithful, who will not suffer you to be tempted above that ye are able; but will with the temptation also make a way to escape, that ye may be able to bear it." He has refused to put more on us than we can bear. We are secure resting in His arms.

Benefits are things that aid or promote wellbeing. Whatever your desires are, begin to name them daily. All it takes is an act of faith to believe that He is well able to perform whatever it is your heart desires. With God nothing is impossible.

Food for thought:

Heavenly benefits are innumerable.

DAY 3

HE CAN HEAR YOU

Reading time: 2 minutes

Devotional Scripture:

"Behold, the Lord's hand is not shortened, that it cannot save; neither his ear heavy, that it cannot hear:" (Isaiah 59:1).

Heart To Heart:

No distraction can hinder Him from making haste to come to your rescue. He is telling us to trust Him. Stop worrying whether He is too busy to save us from our dilemmas, heartaches, and struggles because He is helping others. He is also demonstrating the limitless nature of his power. Lastly, God is letting us know how important our circumstances are to Him. He cares about the small things that rest on our hearts as well as the large things that weigh heavily on our minds.

He wants us to consider the fact that He knows what He is doing 24/7 and He can handle all of it. If we begin to trust the master of our lives, we will gain more ground quicker. Our complete life must be surrendered into His hands. When we willingly place them in His hands, He molds and makes us as the potter does on the potter's wheel. He turns us to the left and the right carefully removing any blotches, nicks, or bubbles. He is the master crafter. If we allow God to do His job without interruption, He does it well.

One key tool we have been blessed with is the ask factor. However, if we refuse to give up our sinful tendencies we can hang it up. We have spiritual perks. Did you know if we live holy according to the scriptures we are privileged to have and receive God's heavenly perks? Ask and receive is in the scriptures. I want all that belongs to me, how about you?

Food for thought:

Even when things seem impossible there is a God who specializes in making it possible.

DAY 4

BEGIN TO COUNT

Reading time: 3 minutes

Devotional Scripture:

"My brethren, count it all joy when ye fall into divers temptations; Knowing this, that the trying of your faith worketh patience." (James 1:2-3)

Heart To Heart:

Our religion has taught us through the years, despite our tumultuous upheavals, to yet have joy. We don't need to pray that God removes our tests and trials. It is more important for us to make the right use of our diverse trials. God works in us through our suffering, creating something good. We don't know everything. We don't have foresight and we are not all knowing.

Our nature doesn't allow us to have knowledge of our future. If that were possible, we would try to plan our lives from A to

Z. It is high time that we begin to count all our many temptations as JOY. Our temptations have been counted as an opportunity to receive joy; they have value. If we were able to look from a different perspective, we would see the true value. What is joy? Joy is something or someone that provides a source of happiness or the emotion of great happiness. If we would begin to rejoice as we trust God during our struggles, God will turn our temptation into deliverance. James 1:4 says, "But let patience have her perfect work, that ye may be perfect and entire, wanting nothing." God is saying that when the temptation comes, we should meet it with joy. What are temptations? He is not implying the temptation of sin or Satan's tactics, but rather the temptations of life such as grief and sorrow. Satan's temptations cannot be counted for joy. If we are tempted by Satan and we indulge, that is sin and sin will bring forth death. In all instances it may not bring forth physical death, but spiritual death.

Food for thought:

The webs we weave may not always be fixable. Be careful.

DAY 5

PEACE IS AVAILABLE

Reading time: 2 minutes

Devotional Scripture:

"Peace I leave with you, my peace I give unto you: not as the world giveth, give I unto you. Let not your heart be troubled, neither let it be afraid." (John 14:27)

Heart To Heart:

Peace is serenity. It is the absence of mental stress, or anxiety. Jesus is stating in this verse that He has peace, and it is available to you. In life we tend to experience dilemmas which cause anxiety and mental stress to grip our hearts. It is not always that we bring it upon ourselves, but sometimes situations happen beyond our control. Jesus - in a nutshell - is saying please don't allow your heart made of blood and veins to become troubled. Heart attacks occur when one or more arteries supplying your heart with oxygen-rich blood become

35

blocked. Stress is a factor which can contribute to an increased risk of having a heart attack.

Do not surround yourself with people who lack. The cliché misery loves company is true. People who suffer from lack of peace will try to contaminate your soul with confusion and disturbances. Block those people from becoming an intricate part of your daily life. When you learn better you will aspire to do better. Surround yourself with people who have an optimistic view of life.

Food for thought:

Your heart is vitally important, so guard, protect and cherish it.

DAY 6

COMMUNICATION WITH GOD

Reading time: 2.5 minutes

Devotional Scripture:

"Call unto me, and I will answer thee, and show thee great and mighty things, which thou knowest not." (Jeremiah 33:3)

Heart To Heart:

This verse is a definite statement. Call means to summon or to make a request. Jesus is saying, "Call My name or summon Me and I will assuredly take the time to answer you." We often call on our families, friends, or associates expecting them to come through for us. But when they fail we are extremely disappointed. Man has frailties. We are an imperfect species. Although we have great intentions, there are times when it is next to impossible for us to do all that we expect of ourselves. Our God is a jealous God. When we neglect Him, He waits for us to call on Him and ask for help. He stands some-

39

where in the shadows watching and waiting. You can recognize Him by the nail prints in His hands. When the enemy shows his face, He lifts a standard against him. We have no valid reason to keep our mouths closed. He desires a verbal relationship with us. He is approachable at all times.

Jeremiah 33:3 challenges us to call to God that He may show us great and mighty things which are unknown to us. Many people in our society are considered brilliant, knowledgeable, and excessively smart. But here Jesus is saying that He is the only one that is omniscient, all-knowing, sagacious, all-seeing, and all-wise. There are things that humans are not privy to. They are great things and mighty things. I would be honored for this Scripture to come to fruition in my life.

Food for thought:

Get wisdom. It prolongs life. In all thy getting, get a clear understanding.

DAY 7

WE HAVE A HEALER

Reading time: 2 minutes

Devotional Scripture:

"He sent his word, and healed them, and delivered them from their destructions." (Psalm 107:20)

Heart To Heart:

Jesus Christ has spoken these words to millions of His people. If we have enough faith to believe His word, God himself will not always have to come. He can send His Word and it accomplishes healing. His Word is so powerful when one is faced with destruction, His Word comes to fruition and delivers with healing power.

His Word is truth so when the truth is stated it erases all lies. Jesus says, "I am the Lord thy God that healeth thee from all sickness and disease." His Word alone is powerful. It is sharper than any two-edged sword. It cuts between the marrow and the bone. Read God's Word. Quote His Word. Believe His Word and watch His Word work for you!

The doctor examines our physical bodies, waits for the test results to come back, and gives a diagnosis. That news can be very scary. The Bible says to be careful how you hear. God wants us to trust Him 100%. Faith brings great results. It may seem preposterous or impossible. But if we can muster enough faith, healing is ours. Regardless of the severity. Even if 99.9% of people with a certain disease have already died, God can send His Word and heal whoever's faith and trust never wavers or falters. Today your healing has arrived.

Food for thought:

Healing is the children's bread.

DAY 8

THE UNRULY MEMBER

Reading time: 2.5 minutes

Devotional Scripture:

"Death and life are in the power of the tongue: and they that love it shall eat the fruit thereof." (Proverbs 18:21)

Heart To Heart:

Without realizing their power, we tend to speak without seasoning our words. As I grow older, I realize the harsh effect our words can have on children, neighbors, friends, enemies, society, and our relatives. As a people we must refrain from the deadly venom that spews out of our mouths. Words cause permanent damage when spoken in a rage. Scripture says life is lived through the spoken word, and death is rendered through the spoken word. This is a warning as well as a wealth of knowledge. The power of life has been given to us. So, it is imperative for us to utilize this power wisely. Death is an uncomfortable subject for most people. But if we

47

could consciously take note of each word that we allow to come up and out, we would choose life instead of death.

Our tongue is one of the smallest parts of our bodies. But the Bible says it is an unruly member. It cannot be tamed. It can be lethal. It is a weapon. Words can murder. The Bible tells us thou shalt not kill. This not only prohibits us from killing someone with a weapon, but also with our untamed words. Just take note of your conversations for at least 7 days and notice the vocabulary you have become accustomed to using. Let's make a commitment to change our verbiage and become a better conversationalist.

Food for thought:

Do unto others as you would have them do to you. Speak daily with tact.

DAY 9

IT'S TIME TO REJOICE

Reading time: 3 minutes

Devotional Scripture:

"This is the day which the Lord hath made; we will rejoice and be glad in it." (Psalm 118:24)

Heart To Heart:

Today can be the best day of your life. Optimistic people never look at what they see and act upon it. Through faith they see it as it is and tweak it so that it turns in their favor. Since the Lord made this day, it has great possibilities. The key to having a blessed day is the art of rejoicing. Praising God for the prospects of your future is what moves God. You do not have to plan naturally. Just begin to rejoice in the spirit and the innumerable manifestations of the supernatural realm of God shall be revealed. Every morning that our eyes are blessed to open is another day the Lord made. We are to rejoice in the simple fact that God has allowed us to experience life for 24 more hours. As we grow older and begin to realize how blessed we are to be alive and that it is only by the grace of God, I believe our praise will shift to a higher dimension.

I believe our worship will expand to a higher level and the doors which have been closed tight will begin to open for us as the jail cell opened for Peter in Acts 12. Peter slept between two soldiers. He was bound with two chains and there were keepers of the prison standing guard and watching over the prison. Prayer was made around the clock and an angel of the Lord appeared. A light shone in the prison and the angel smote Peter on the side and raised him up. As he rejoiced, his chains fell off. You may wonder what one gets out of rejoicing. I would venture to say anything your heart desires. Stop what you are doing right now and begin to rejoice in the Lord.

Food for thought:

Rejoicing causes swift deliverance.

DAY 10

THE EARTH BELONGS TO GOD

Reading time: 2.5 minutes

Devotional Scripture:

"The earth is the Lord's, and the fulness thereof; the world, and they that dwell therein." (Psalm 24:1)

Heart To Heart:

The earth belongs to God and everything that is in it. All the money and everything that money can buy belongs to God. It is imperative that we ask ourselves a very poignant question. Am I representing Christ well by the choices I am making daily? We must live a life that is pleasing to God who is the master source of our being. To receive all that God has planned for us, we must conduct ourselves the way Scripture - our roadmap - has directed us to.

We belong to God. Yes! Every person on the face of the earth, red, yellow, black and white has a father and it is God. He has allowed us to live on His earth as He did the first man and woman, Adam and Eve. The Garden of Eden was furnished with abundance of all that was ever needed for them to survive. Since Eve allowed the serpent to speak to her, she responded to him, and finally obeyed him by eating and sharing the forbidden fruit from the tree of knowledge of good and evil with Adam, we are now recipients of the consequences of their disobedience. This Scripture is our garden. We can tap into whatever we need. If we ask anything according to His will, we shall have it. If we are lacking in any area, we must study the Word because it is our instructions for living on the earth. We must obey.

Food for thought:

Let's go back to Eden and flourish.

DAY 11

IT'S TIME TO SING AND WORSHIP THE LORD

Reading time: 1.5 minutes

Devotional Song:

The Storm is Passing Over

Sing Unto The Lord:

> *O courage, my soul, and let us journey on,*
> *For though' the night is dark, it won't be very long.*
> *O thanks be to God, the morning light appears,*
> *And the storm is passing over, Hallelujah!*

Refrain:

Hallelujah! Hallelujah!
The storm is passing over,
Hallelujah!

O billows rolling high, and thunder shakes the ground,
The lightning's flash, and tempest all around,
But Jesus walks the sea and calms the angry waves,
And the storm is passing over, Hallelujah!

Refrain:

The stars have disappeared, and distant lights are dim,
My soul is filled with fears, the seas are breaking in.
I hear the Master cry, "Be not afraid, 'tis I,"
And the storm is passing over, Hallelujah!

Now soon we shall reach the distant shining shore,
Then free from all the storms, we'll rest forevermore.
And safe within the veil, we'll furl the riven sail,
And the storm will all be over, Hallelujah!

Food for thought:

Never lose your heart-song!

DAY 12

MY DAILY AFFIRMATIONS

Reading time: 1.5 minutes

Devotional Scripture:

"I had fainted, unless I had believed to see the goodness of the Lord in the land of the living." (Psalm 27:13)

Heart To Heart:

I am phenomenal.

I am draped and clothed with wisdom.

I have the fear, love, and knowledge of God.

My business is a blessing to many people.

Clients reach out to me and are abundantly blessed.

My productivity is massive.

My income will double, triple, and supersede my wildest imagination this year!

God has shifted my life and a great turn around is quickly happening!

I am the head and not the tail.

I am the lender and not the borrower.

There will be no lack, no loss, and no liability in my life.

I am healthy, wealthy, and wise.

My body and my mind are whole.

Nothing and nobody can hinder the plans of God.

My family is an asset, my children are an asset,

and I am an asset.

I am set for abundant life according to the Scriptures.

Food for thought:

Never forget who you really are. Love yourself. You are important.

DAY 13

PIECES

Reading time: 3 minutes

Devotional Scripture:

"Know ye that the Lord he is God: it is he that hath made us, and not we ourselves; we are his people, and the sheep of his pasture." (Psalm 100:3)

Heart To Heart:

Our human bodies are made up of many molecules. As I sat here before work, a thought came to my mind. "Does anyone really know who we are as individuals?" The answer came back with resounding force. "No!" "Why not?" you may ask. Well, there are a variety of elements involved. There are sides to our personality that we only allow certain people to really know. We are made up of many pieces. Do we allow everyone in on our various pieces or do we save certain ones for certain people? Do we share our huge personalities with strangers or co-workers? Or do we spread them out depending on the situation? Does anyone really know you? If not, why? Are you afraid that if you were to be yourself, they would not like you? Or is it that you don't like yourself? Maybe you haven't taken the time out to learn all about yourself? Or are you embarrassed to show your true, raw, real self to the public?

I love people, all people. I find that if a person is warm like me, I feel more comfortable to openly share my complete personality. I must say that everyone who gets a chance to witness my raw personality loves it. On the other hand, if I happen to run into a snobbish, self-centered, cold-hearted individual, I feel like I'm not going to waste my God-given personality on them. So, I clam up and begin observing and listening. These seem to be tools I use as a defense mechanism. People with abusive personalities tend to hurt or try to damage others' egos or self-esteem. Therefore, I am on my guard right away and I will never reveal my bright personality. Why? Because when people are out to get you, wisdom must prevail and it is not time for war. It is a true saying, "Hurting people, hurt, others." I have witnessed this repeatedly, and, as I view this avalanche, it is not a pretty picture.

Food for thought:

Persecuted but not forsaken, cast down but not destroyed.

DAY 14

DON'T BE AFRAID TO LOVE - PART 1

Reading time: 2 minutes

Devotional Scripture:

"Though I speak with the tongues of men and of angels, and have not charity, I am become as sounding brass, or a tinkling cymbal." (1 Corinthians 13:1)

Heart To Heart:

(1st fruit of the spirit) 1 Corinthians 13:1-7

1 Though I speak with the tongues of men and of angels, and have not charity, I am become as sounding brass, or a tinkling cymbal.

2 And though I have the gift of prophecy, and understand all mysteries, and all knowledge; and though I have all faith, so that I could remove mountains, and have not charity, I am nothing.

3 And though I bestow all my goods to feed the poor, and though I give my body to be burned, and have not charity, it profiteth me nothing.

4 Charity suffereth long, and is kind; charity envieth not; charity vaunteth not itself, is not puffed up,

5 Doth not behave itself unseemly, seeketh not her own, is not easily provoked, thinketh no evil.

6 Rejoiceth not in iniquity, but rejoiceth in the truth.

7 Beareth all things, believeth all things, hopeth all things, endureth all things.

Food for thought:

Love is more than a choice, love is more than a feeling, love is a decision!

DAY 15

DON'T BE AFRAID TO LOVE - PART 2

Reading time: 2.5 minutes

Devotional Scripture:

"But the fruit of the Spirit is love, joy, peace, longsuffering, gentleness, goodness, faith, Meekness, temperance: against such there is no law." (Galatians 5:22-23)

Heart To Heart:

Love is God and God is love. Webster's dictionary defines love as

1. Having a profoundly tender, passionate affection for another person.

2. A feeling of warm personal attachment or deep affection, as for a parent, child, or a friend.

The Scriptures have the best description of the true meaning of love. So, as we further discuss 1 Corinthians 13:1-8 on days 15 through 18 of this book, it will give a clearer understanding of what God is expecting of all of us.

A. LOVE IS PATIENT. Verse 4 - (Long suffering). Even when you feel like forcefully expressing yourself. Love bears pain without complaint, shows forbearance under provocation or strain, and is steadfast despite opposition, difficulty, or adversity.

B. LOVE IS KIND. Verse 4 - Even when you want to retaliate physically or tear down another with your words. Love is sympathetic, considerate, gentle, and agreeable. It causes one to use tact.

C. LOVE IS NOT JEALOUS. Verse 4 - It envieth not, especially when one is aware that others are being noticed more than oneself. Love does not participate at all in rivalry, is not hostile toward others, and is not suspicious. Love works for the welfare and good of others.

D. LOVE DOES NOT BRAG. Verse 4 - It vaunteth not itself, even when you want to tell the world about your accomplishments. Love does not flaunt itself boastfully and does not engage in self-glorification. Instead, love lifts and builds up others, it is not braggadocious in any way.

E.   LOVE IS NOT ARROGANT. Verse 4 -It is not puffed up, even when you think you are right, and others are wrong. Love does not assert itself or become aggressive in dealing with others.

Food for thought:

Love is God and God is love.

DAY 16

DON'T BE AFRAID TO LOVE –
PART 3

Reading time: 3 minutes

Devotional Scripture:

"Love not the world, neither the things that are in the world. If any man love the world, the love of the Father is not in him." (1 John 2:15)

Heart To Heart:

F. LOVE DOES NOT ACT UNBECOMINGLY. Verse 5 - It does not behave itself unseemly, even when being boastful, rude, or overbearing will get you attention and allow you to get your own way. Love conforms to what is right, not adjusting to what is wrong. Love searches out how one would honor the Lord.

G. LOVE DOES NOT SEEK ITS OWN. Verse 5 - Biblical love is neither selfish nor self-seeking. True love does not try to fulfill its own desires, does not ask for its own way, and does not try to acquire or gain for itself. Love is an act of the will which seeks to be a servant; not to be served.

H. LOVE IS NOT PROVOKED. Verse 5 - Even when others attempt to provoke you, or you are tempted to strike out at something or someone. Love is not aroused or incited to outbursts of anger. Love continues faithfully and gently to train others in righteousness, even when they fail. One cannot say as justification, "But they provoked me and if they had left me alone things would have never escalated to that level." Love is not ugly.

I. LOVE DOES NOT REJOICE IN UNRIGHTEOUSNESS. Verse 6 - It rejoiceth not in iniquity. Even when it seems like a misfortune is the reward for their previous actions, love mourns over sin, its effects and the pain which results from living in a fallen world. Love seeks to reconcile others with the Lord. Love shows active compassion.

Food for thought:

There is accountability in true love.

DAY 17

DON'T BE AFRAID TO LOVE - PART 4

Reading time: 3 minutes

Devotional Scripture:

"A new commandment I give unto you, That ye love one another; as I have loved you, that ye also love one another." (John 13:34)

Heart To Heart:

K. LOVE REJOICES WITH THE TRUTH. Verse 6 - Even when it seems easier and more beneficial to lie. Love is joyful when truth is known, even when it may lead to adverse circumstances, reviling, and persecution. Even when one feels threatened to lie because of the strict punishment they may receive.

L. LOVE BEARS ALL THINGS. Verse 7 - Even when disappointments seem overwhelming. Love is tolerant, endures with others who are difficult to understand or deal with, and has an unending internal and external dialogue of difficulties. Love remembers that God develops spiritual maturity through difficult circumstances and that it had to go through the hands and fingers of Jesus to be approved before it came to us. Love knows at the end it will all work out for our good.

M. LOVE BELIEVES ALL THINGS. Verse 7 - Even when others' actions are ambiguous, and you feel like not trusting anyone. Love remains trusting, does not judge people's motives, and believes others until facts prove contrary. Yes, even when facts prove that the other person is untrustworthy, love seeks to help restore the other's character back to trustworthiness.

N. LOVE HOPES ALL THINGS. Verse 7 - Even when nothing appears to be going right, on the inside or the outside. Love expects fulfillment of God's plan and sits and anticipates the best outcome for the other person. Love confidently entrusts others to the Lord to do His sovereign, permissive and perfect will in their lives.

O. LOVE ENDURES ALL THINGS. Verse 7 - All means all. This may be one of the hardest qualities to practice. When you think you just can't tolerate the people or circumstances in your life any longer, love remains steadfast regardless.

Food for thought:

The unlimited love of God has no boundaries!

DAY 18

DON'T BE AFRAID TO LOVE - PART 5

Reading time: 2.5 minutes

Devotional Scripture:

"A friend loveth at all times, and a brother is born for adversity." (Proverbs 17:17)

Heart To Heart:

If you don't give in during times of suffering and hardship you will yield good returns.

P. LOVE NEVER FAILS. Verse 8 - Even when you feel overwhelmed, overly stressed, and hopeless, love will not crumble under pressure or difficulties. Love remains faithful even to the point of death. It utilizes grace.

Love is like the energizer bunny; it keeps giving and giving even though it may not see the harvest.

Love is not based on emotion or feeling. It is based on action. It endures through the storms and the rain, through the vehement winds and the Euroclydon winds. It yet endures through midnight tears, sorrow, and grief. Love doesn't offer an option button that switches on and off. It is steadfast. It remains intact throughout life's trying times. Remember the saying, "love is stronger than death."

This quote is true. Let me share my heart with you concerning a very touching subject. One of my dear sisters got deathly ill and the doctors called our large family into a private room to share her condition with this disclaimer: Love is stronger than death. Your daughter, your sister, your aunt is staying alive solely because of the love your family has shown her during this phase of her life. He stated, "Let her go. She is suffering and it's not good." It was the most difficult thing to ask a blood relative to do. But, under the circumstances, if we genuinely loved her, we would be willing to do what was best for her even if it hurt us. At the end of the day, we were able to release her so she could go live with the one who ultimately loved her best.

Food for thought:

Love is stronger than death!

DAY 19

JOY

Reading time: 3 minutes

Devotional Scripture:

"Weeping may endure for a night, but joy cometh in the morning." (Psalm 30:5b)

Heart To Heart:

This thing called life! There are certain things that come along with life; weeping for instance. Crying is a part of the totality of life nobody has prepared to handle. There are no instructions or manuals to easily guide us through the vicissitudes of life.

Things often seem worse at night. When one is attacked with a sickness, illness, or affliction, things seem to be exacerbated in the still and darkness. I suffered with asthma as a child and many nights the thought crossed my mind that this would be the fatal night. I remember that in the 80's my parents were strict in their faith and they didn't believe in medicine at all so when I had an attack, they would pray. This night my symptoms progressed worse and fear began to set in. My sister Cynthia got scared enough to summon my parents. I recall my mom and dad coming into the room. One knelt on either side of my comfortable queen-sized bed and they began to pray the effectual fervent prayer of the righteous. It was their faith that would help me through this dilemma. My dad left to get his Bible - his King James Version. He firmly stood by this and this alone. When he reentered the room, he began reading from the Book of Job 33:4 which states, "The spirit of God hath made me, and the breath of the Almighty has given me life." He said, "Whenever you feel yourself laboring in your breathing, quote this Scripture and God will heal your lungs." I trusted his words and quoted the Scripture until I fell asleep. When I awoke the next morning, my breathing was back to normal. The latter clause of the devotional scripture states, "joy cometh in the morning." I am a living testament and I now believe in divine healing with all my heart. God will send joy unspeakable and full of glory. He has done it for me all my life.

Food for thought:

Joy is attainable if you pursue it!

DAY 20

PEACE

Reading time: 3 minutes

Devotional Scripture:

"Great peace have they which love thy law: and nothing shall offend them." (Psalm 119:165)

Heart To Heart:

(3rd fruit of the spirit)

Trivia: The longest chapter in the Bible is Psalm 119. The shortest chapter in the Bible is Psalm 117. Furthermore, the middle or center of the Bible is Psalms 118.

Peace is defined as the absence of hostility or rage, or a personality free of internal or external strife. Peace is attainable although we witness the opposite daily with displays of war, murder, rape, molestation, physical, mental, financial, spiritual, emotional, and verbal abuse in the media. We must realize that healing is required in these situations before being able to experience peace and serenity.

Peace can be subjective based on one's age, environment, or experiences. Peace to a fourteen-year-old, for example, may mean something different from the definition given by an eight-year-old. I had the opportunity to interview a child in both age groups. The fourteen-year-old said, "It means to be one with yourself." The eight-year-old said, "It means to have a quiet atmosphere."

Both descriptions are true as there are many forms of peace and if you reach your pinnacle or height of peace, you will thrive. Peace is contagious. I find that when someone who truly exhibits peace is in a room, the entire ambiance of the room adjusts to that attitude.

The opposite of peace is disturbance, which means to exhibit behaviors that are not appropriate for a healthy environment. There is a famous quote that I remember from a little girl. "Misery loves company." I have had the unfortunate chance to witness many miserable people in my life and I often wonder why they are so miserable. I see life as a gift and I'm always ecstatic when God wakes me every morning. He greets me with brand new mercies and fresh opportunities to be more creative, to do things better tomorrow than I did yesterday or even today.

Food for thought:

Peace can come even in a whirlwind.

DAY 21

LIVE LIFE

Reading time: 6 minutes

Devotional Scripture:

"Ask, and it shall be given you; seek, and ye shall find; knock, and it shall be opened unto you:" (Matthew 7:7)

Heart To Heart:

I believe there is a great misconception regarding the enjoyment of life. I also feel like we don't really know what it means to live, to thrive, and to love life. A few years ago, I had the opportunity to travel to Puerto Rico with my baby sister. I learned some important things about life.

On one occasion, while on a guided tour, I observed people from all over the world as they walked to and fro looking at the awe-inspiring beauty of this earth. I watched the elderly walk up the largest staircase in the world. Seeing their eyes beaming with excitement gave me joy. I realized what they were doing. They were making time to enjoy life. I vividly remember the tour guide jumping into a body of water. He picked up a pebble and slid it across a rock. The color was bright green. To my surprise, he threw that one back and picked up another pebble. He slid it across the large rock, and it was bright red. Another one was bright purple. His decision to jump into the water and allow the tourists to bear witness to the beautiful colors of God's creations added another layer of enjoyment to the experience. Oh, we must take the time to live and enjoy the beauty of life.

In order to live we must slow our pace mentally, emotionally, physically, and spiritually. We live as though we are in a race to do everything. Excuse my vernacular, but we rush around like a chicken with its head cut off. We rush to work, we rush home, we rush to eat, we rush to sleep, we rush to speak, and we rarely are available for silence. Seldom do we take advantage of opportunities to sit and appreciate the stillness. We impatiently wait at the red light, it cannot change fast enough for us. The stop sign interrupts our flow, and we have no patience to listen or wait in line because we are so wired. God is giving us a chance to slow down and enjoy the beauty of life.

God wants His children to make time to enjoy His creation that He made for us. While on this magnificent trip, I had the opportunity to see God in His glory. I learned how to appreciate God as we waited in line. I turned my head to the right and water poured out of a huge rock. It was the most beautiful waterfall you ever wanted to see. I stood there in awe of God. He strategically designed every mountain. Every grain of sand was made exactly right, and the colors were made in the perfect hue. He was intentional about the shade of every rock as well. God's expertise in brightness and contrast and the colors I saw could not be duplicated by man. It was remarkable to see the ocean as rippling waves rose to such a level, but the bank never overflowed. God allowed me the opportunity to see His creation and for that I am grateful.

I wonder if you can learn how to slow down day by day and step by step. There is a whole world out there that we have never imagined in our wildest dreams. I am a person who finds enjoyment in taking walks. I remember as I raised my children it was challenging to find time to go on walks. One day, as I found a window of time to rush out of the house for a walk, I accelerated to a fast pace as if I were jogging. I rushed what was meant to be enjoyable. I rushed past houses, plazas, and cars. If I were asked the color, the size, or the name of the stores, I wouldn't be able to come up with the answers because I was too busy trying to finish before I began. As I walked, something in my mind said, "SLOW DOWN!" I felt my pace quickly change and, as I looked to my left-hand side, there was a flower bed full of beautiful, multicolored flowers. I bent over and smelled the aroma that only God can make. That day changed my life. Now I try to look deeper and take the time to enjoy things and people that I wouldn't ordinarily have paid attention to.

If God ever grants the opportunity for you to travel, go! Don't try to figure it all out. Don't try to organize things to perfection on a human level. Do not be so quick to say, "I can't go" or ",I don't have the necessary funds". Don't say "the time isn't right" or "I can't go alone." Just go!

Food for thought:

Don't hesitate to take in the complete view and live life to the fullest.

DAY 22

DOUBT, FEAR, AND UNBELIEF

Reading time: 2.5 minutes

Devotional Scripture:

"There is no fear in love; but perfect love casteth out fear: because fear hath torment. He that feareth is not made perfect in love." (1 John 4:18)

Heart To Heart:

These three attributes are from a force that means us no good. Doubt is a delusion which stems from fear. Fear is false evidence that the enemy has made to appear real. And finally, unbelief is the lack of faith.

When our best is going to be uncovered, the enemy rises to the occasion and stirs up a plan to defeat us. Doubt, fear, and unbelief are tools he uses to stop us in our tracks. He tries to make us doubt the Word of God, our leaders, our parents, our elders, our mentors, and our complete infrastructure.

Doubt, fear, and unbelief begin in the mind. I admonish you to protect your thoughts. Do not allow your mind to wander or daydream too long. I also admonish you to be careful what you hear. Protect your ear gates. Don't listen to everything and everybody. Your eyes play an important part as well. Be cautious about what you allow in your view. I must warn you to watch the places you go. Protect your walk with God and choose wisely where you go and who you take with you. Be careful of the company you keep. My words of caution may remind you of your youth when your parents instructed you with a long list of dos and don'ts, butI'm speaking from my heart. I pray that you listen, take heed, and remember as the Scripture clearly states, that warning cometh before destruction.

Food for thought:

The illusions of the enemy are only traps, therefore trust God 24/7.

DAY 23

OH, GIVE THANKS UNTO THE LORD FOR HE IS GOD!

Reading time: 4 minutes

Devotional Scripture:

"O give thanks unto the Lord, for he is good: for his mercy endureth for ever." (Psalm 107:1)

Heart To Heart:

Having a heart full of gratitude is rewarding. When one can count their blessings and name them one by one, God recognizes that and grants many blessings in return. Sometimes life happens and we feel like we are in a rut. Our circumstances become as a ton of bricks that have been thrown at us to crush our entire being. We must remember that God knows every one of our tests and trials and He will deliver us out of them all. Deliverance will be on time, every time. It is imperative for us to count our blessings daily and to not lose sight of all the Lord has done for us even in the midst of hardship. This applies to the small things as well as the large things.

If you would do an exercise with me, I believe you will be enlightened and filled with a thankful heart, mind, and soul. Place one hand over your nose just for 30 seconds and keep your mouth closed. Now, how long has it been since you thanked Him for the breath in your nostrils? Place both of your hands over your ears. How long has it been since you thanked Him for the ability to hear? Look at your knees, your legs, and your toes. How long has it been since you thanked Him for the ability to walk? Raise your hands. How long has it been since you thanked Him for the activity of your limbs? He could have, just for a split second, judged us on the simple fact that we are guilty of a whole lot of things and let us suffer in agony and in pain. But God is awesome even when we, a spoiled people, complain, sin, and throw temper tantrums. His grace is sufficient. His grace is amazing.

He makes a point to let us know that, despite our lack of faithfulness, He will remain faithful. He shows His agape love twenty-four seven. Human nature gives us a sense of entitlement and a mindset that the world owes us something. But the truth is we owe a debt that we can never afford to repay. Our debt is enormous. If God wanted to, He could judge us according to our daily sins, but in His awesomeness, He shows His ability to love. Despite our selfishness, He chooses to love us. Despite our ways of error and condescending thoughts, He has made a permanent decision to love us. Despite our rebellion and disobedience. Despite our ugly disposition, He has already made us know through His birth, death, burial, dissension, resurrection, and ascension that His love is *Agape* love. Permanent love. Everlasting love.

The type of love that nobody can take away from us. He has taken our huge debt and paid it in full with His innocent blood.

Food for thought:

Do not revere God as we would man. Give Him His complete worth.

DAY 24

FAITH

Reading time: 2 minutes

Devotional Scripture:

"But grow in grace, and in the knowledge of our Lord and Saviour Jesus Christ. To him be glory both now and for ever. Amen." (2 Peter 3:18)

Heart To Heart:

(7th Fruit of the Spirit)

Every human heartbeat pumps the words *grow, grow, grow*. Every planted seed is saying "grow, grow, grow." If you listen to every newborn baby born into the world, their heartbeat is saying "grow, grow, grow." God has deposited wisdom, knowledge, intellect, and creativity inside of us that is begging and screaming to be unlocked.

Today is your day to envision the dreams of your future because they will come to pass when you act upon your dreams. Your dreams will grow larger than you can imagine. I am excited about your future. Are you?

All of Heaven is backing you. You have done well, but there is more inside of you that must come to fruition. The trouble has been great. The disappointment can't be minimized, but it has only come to make you stronger for the glory of God and for the benefit of others. Push through the darkest of circumstances and the prize at the end will be rewarding.

Food for thought:

You are standing under an open heaven.

DAY 25

GOODNESS

Reading time: 6 minutes

Devotional Scripture:

"But the fruit of the Spirit is love, joy, peace, longsuffering, gentleness, goodness, faith, Meekness, temperance: against such there is no law." (Galatians 5:22-23)

Heart To Heart:

There are nine qualities of growth that God wants us to utilize to better prepare us for the kingdom. Goodness is the 6th fruit of the spirit and it is an immensely powerful testament to the favor, blessing, and comforting effects of the absolutes of God's written Word. It is an absolute statement that goodness and mercy shall follow me all the days of my life and I will dwell in the house of the Lord forever.

God is showing His willingness and freedom to follow us through the vicissitudes of life regardless of the tumultuous ups and downs we encounter year in and year out. We have an advocate who stands ready to fend for us 24/7. All we must do is obey. Jeremiah 33:3 states, "Call unto me and I will answer thee and show thee great and mighty things, which thou knowest not."

It is good to be good and it is kind to be kind. We all have an obligation to be good. But not everyone obeys the unwritten rule. Apostle Paul states that when he would do good evil was always present. Doing good is cathartic and beneficial to one's health and wellbeing. Abraham Lincoln said, "When I do good, I feel good. When I do bad, I feel bad, and that's my religion." His quote is self-explanatory, and it applies to everyone. I wish doing good for others gave us a straight passage into Heaven, but that is not the case. Heaven is a place where we must obey the commandments, laws, principles, and precepts of the written Word of God in order to be worthy of a seat within the pearly gates.

God has freely given us goodness and mercy which are the set of twins I cherish. They go hand in hand. As a reward, He allows goodness and mercy to follow us to our places of employment, on the airplane, in the mountains, in the desert, on vacation, at the doctor's appointment, operating rooms, courtrooms, and in front of the unjust judge. He will not drop the ball when you are in trouble. He will secure you and bring you out on the side of victory. God will stick with you throughout the ebbs and flows of life with distinct pleasure. One Scripture that has carried me through my toughest times of life is, "The Lord passed before him and proclaimed, 'The Lord, the Lord God merciful and gracious, slow to anger, and abounding in steadfast love and faithfulness, keeping steadfast love for thousands, forgiving iniquity and transgression and sin.'" (Exodus 34: 6-7) The divine presence of God is referred to as the Shekinah glory of God. It abides, dwells, encompasses, it resides, rests, and permanently stays with us. Cherish His demonstrations of love that He so faithfully gives through our day, weeks, months, and years. Show appreciation and spread the Word to others so that His glory will not be in vain.

Spreading the message of Jesus Christ is our main purpose for living on the face of the earth. If we stay behind the four walls of our homes in our comfort zone, we are outside the will of God. God wants His people to be disciples like the 12 in Matthew's Gospel. The names of the apostles chosen were Simon, Andrew, James son of Zebedee, his brother, John, Philip, Bartholomew, Thomas, Matthew the tax collector, James son of Alphaeus, Thaddaeus, Simon the Zealot, and Judas Iscariot who betrayed Jesus.

Jesus instructed these men not to go among the Gentiles or enter any town of the Samaritans. Jesus said, "Go rather to the lost sheep of Israel. As you go, preach this message; the kingdom of heaven is near. Heal the sick, raise the dead, cleanse those who have leprosy, drive out demons. Freely you have received, freely give." We all have a day of reckoning and I remind you that it is upon the horizon. Jesus will sound His trumpet, the dead in Christ will rise first, and they that remain shall be caught up together in the air.

Food for thought:

We ALL have the same assignment, and we are behind the eight ball as the rapture is soon to come.

DAY 26

LONGSUFFERING

Reading time: 3 minutes

Devotional Scripture:

"Put on therefore, as the elect of God, holy and beloved, bowels of mercies, kindness, humbleness of mind, meekness, longsuffering;" (Colossians 3:12)

Heart To Heart:

The fourth fruit of the spirit is long-suffering. This is a unique word that is used sparingly today. It is an adjective. The description given in Webster's Dictionary described as; having or showing patience despite troubles, especially those caused by other people. Having the ability to deal with troubling issues with people and situations even though things are not completely favorable.

When we take on new employment, the excitement tops the charts. We go in without preconceived notions and we are excit-

127

ed about our new assignments. We are eager to start work at our new, amazing job. So, we arrive early, set everything up before the boss arrives, then, without realizing it, within a month or two we may regret the day we filled out the application. We curse the day they called us in for an interview, the moment they sent the acceptance letter, and the first day we arrived on the grounds of said "amazing" job. Why? Let's picture this: our boss is now against us and causes our days and weeks to seem like months and years. We now dread waking up because this is no longer our passion. It's no longer a place that welcomes us with open arms. It has now become our nemesis.

Even when we are put in a comfortable place, we must remain focused on the plan and the will of God to endure hardness as a good soldier of the Lord Jesus Christ. Hold on to your integrity and pray without ceasing. God will wrap you up in a soft blanket and lead you to your next phase. Either He will steer the ship and allow you to stay or He will lead you to your next assignment. Clarity of His will is what I want you to pray for.

Food for thought:

Lord, I thank you for clarity, guidance, wisdom, and knowledge for my next move. In Jesus name, Amen.

DAY 27

STORMS

Reading time: 10 minutes

Devotional Scripture:

"And we know that all things work together for good to them that love God, to them who are the called according to his purpose." (Romans 8:28)

Heart To Heart:

> When fear and worry test your faith
> And anxious thoughts assail,
> Remember God is in control
> And He will never fail.
> -Sper

L ook at Jesus as He calms the storm. "And when he entered the ship, his disciples followed him. And behold, there arose a great tempest in the sea, insomuch that the ship was covered with the waves; but he was asleep. And his disciples came to him, and awoke him, saying, Lord, save us; we perish. And he saith unto them, Why are ye fearful, O ye of little faith? Then he arose and rebuked the winds and the sea; and there was a great calm. But the men marveled, saying, "What manner of man is this, that even the winds and the sea obey him!?" (Matthew 8:23-27)

We too will experience major challenges in our daily lives. It is then that we must get in the face of God and cry out, "Oh God, it is me! Help me! Deliver me! Calm the storms that rage in my life." We must get His attention just like the disciples did in the Bible days. Wake Jesus up and say, "Master, carest thou not that we perish?" He can be touched with the feelings of our infirmities. He understands what we go through daily and He wants us to know that we have an advocate that can get to God for us and His name is Jesus of Nazareth.

There are a few more names we can use when describing our Savior; the Lion of the Tribe of Judah, the Root of David, the Seed of Abraham, the Rock hewn out of the mountain, the meek and humble Lamb. I call Him Jesus, my Rock in a weary land. What do you call Him? Know that you are not alone on your journey. You have someone fighting for you and advocating for your success, your health, your family, your home, your employment, etc. It may seem as though you have no one on your side, that you are all alone, that no one really cares about your wellbeing, and that you have no worth, or purpose.

I come to defend the gospel of Jesus Christ to let you know that there is someone that sits high and looks down low. He looks from left to right and scans the universe. He is our creator and He not only cares about your wellbeing, but He is compassionate about numbering the strands of hair on your head. He cares about the blood that runs warm in your veins. He cares about the crashing thoughts that infiltrate your mind. He cares about the inner dialogue taking place in the secret places of your residence. Yes, He loves every inch of your being and He reminds us in His Word, "For I know the plans I have for you, declares the Lord, plans to prosper you and not to harm you, plans to give you hope and a future." (Jeremiah 29:11)

The disciples depended on Jesus to deliver them and He did. We can also personally call Him and watch Him deliver us. He is no respecter of persons. He has no favorites. He has no nepotism. No, God is a just, fair, and kind God who loves everyone just the same. He says, "Come unto me all ye that labor and are heavy laden and I will give you rest." He includes everyone and excludes no one. Will you share your experience of Christ with others? That is how His name can be spread throughout the universe. Tell someone that He is a healer and a deliverer. I was in trouble and no one could deliver me, but God sent help and now I am free. Our assignment is to tell of His goodness.

I was diagnosed with a terrible disease and the doctors didn't know what to do for me. So, I prayed and asked God to heal me and show the path for my life. I trusted God to heal me as He has done for others, but my path and journey has been different. Yours may be different. You may even be going through the same thing and need to hear someone say you're going to make it.

In 2016 I received news. I don't call it bad news because it has taught me many excellent lessons, I would not have learned had I not experienced this. I didn't act upon it until 2018 at the end of the year after the dream vacation I had promised my children. They were ecstatic we were flying to Florida! I saved the money as a single, divorced mother of multiple children and paid for the plane tickets. I paid for the immaculate rental resort private home. I paid for everything I could think of and we had an amazing trip. Daily I went on the Lazy River in Champions Gate and talked with God. It was peaceful. I went on long walks while the children were asleep. I took pictures to capture the moments and went back to take a shower. I stepped out of the shower and I heard a voice say to me, "You will not have to go through all that others have gone through." I was shocked. I said, "Explain what you are saying." He repeated Himself and a presence overshadowed me. I didn't understand what he meant but I trusted what he said to me. I sat down to ponder what had just happened, and I began to praise and worship God and speak in my heavenly language. I then laid down on my comfortable pillows, covered myself up, and fell into a deep peaceful sleep in my king-sized bed.

We stayed for a week in Orlando and enjoyed every minute of God's wonderful sunshine. I did not want to return home because of all the challenges I had left behind. I was able to leave every trouble behind me, even the news of my health.

My dear sister flew in and stayed with me in the beautiful vacation home. My Goddaughter and family lived close by. They brought food over as we fellowshipped and enjoyed a few laughs. We went to the movies for her daughter's birthday and went out to dinner. We all enjoyed ourselves because we hadn't seen each other in many years. Her children were all grown up, married with their own children. Now we were able to see her grandchildren. That was a lot of fun for me as I took great interest in her ability to raise her children. Now her grands have taken the stage. One of my friends, Erin, drove to meet me and spent the night with me. We went out to dinner and reminisced into the wee hours of the morning. I enjoyed my God given vacation. On the last day our Uber came to the house to pick us up and take us to the airport. It was bittersweet of course, but we can't ignore our circumstances. We must deal with them and face our worst fears. On day 32, I will provide more of my present circumstances with hopes it will strengthen your faith and walk with God. He cares about you from the days of inception until the day you meet Him face to face.

Food for thought:

Face your worst fears head-on. You do not have to fear.

DAY 28

HEARTACHE

Reading time: 3 minutes

Devotional Scripture:

"Fear thou not; for I am with thee: be not dismayed; for I am thy God: I will strengthen thee; yea, I will help thee; yea, I will uphold thee with the right hand of my righteousness." (Isaiah 41:10)

Heart To Heart:

God sympathizes with your heartache!

In Matthew, Jesus healed two demon-possessed men. These men were violent and had the town scared to pass by where they were. One day the demons shouted out loud, "What do you want with us, Son of God?" They went on to say, "Have you come here to torture us before the appointed time?" In the distance a large herd of pigs were feeding. The demons begged Jesus, "If you drive us out, send us into the herd of pigs." He said to them, "Go!" So, they came out and went into the pigs. The entire herd rushed down the steep bank into the lake and died in the water. Those tending the pigs ran off, went into the town and reported all this, including what had happened to the demon-possessed man. The whole town went out to meet Jesus., and when they saw Him, they pleaded with Him to leave their region.

Satan's demons come on the scene to torment, to cause pain, misery, sadness, sorrow, depression, low self-esteem, isolation, division, separation, loss, heartache, disease, trouble, unemployment, lack of income, and unhealthy relationships. The Devil has a limited time for his assignment. Therefore, he leaves no stone unturned. He does not have prejudice. He does not care about the color of your skin, your age, background, ethnicity, class, or legacy. He wants everyone he can get. God comes to shed light on everything and everyone. God comes to save, heal, deliver, set the captive free. Those who are bound He delivers them immediately. He has a plan for your life to prosper you and not harm you. But first, you must believe.

Food for thought:

Life is too short only to exist. Embrace God's beauty. It is amazing.

DAY 29

JESUS FEEDS 5,000

Reading time: 1 minute

Devotional Scripture:

"When Jesus heard of it, he departed thence by ship into a desert place apart: and when the people had heard thereof, they followed him on foot out of the cities." (Matthew 14:13)

Heart To Heart:

John the Baptist was beheaded. Now after John's disciples came and took his body to be buried, they went and told Jesus what happened. And when Jesus heard about His cousin He went privately to a solitary place. The crowd followed Him, and it was getting dark. So, His disciples asked Jesus to send the crowd away because soon they would get hungry and there was not enough food in this isolated place. Jesus replied, "No. They do not need to go away. You give them something to eat." They explained that all they had was a little lad's lunch which consisted of two fish and five barley loaves of bread. Jesus replied, "Bring them to me." He directed the people to have a seat on the grass. He took the five loaves of bread and two fish, looked up to Heaven, gave thanks, and broke it. Then He gave them to the disciples, and the disciples gave them to the people. They all ate and were satisfied. And the disciples picked up the 12 baskets of broken pieces that were leftover. The number of those who ate was about five thousand men besides women and children.

Just like Jesus immediately made preparation for the crowd, He is planning your future as well. He is preparing a table before you in the presence of your enemies. He is establishing a way of escape for your finances. He is making the enemy leave your health alone. Trust the process.

Food for thought:

Even when you can't understand it, just trust it. He always hits the bullseye.

DAY 30

GOD'S REQUEST FOR HIS PEOPLE

Reading time: 1 minute

Devotional Scripture:

"If my people, which are called by my name, shall humble themselves, and pray, and seek my face, and turn from their wicked ways; then will I hear from heaven, and will forgive their sin, and will heal their land." (2 Chronicles 7:14)

Heart To Heart:

If my people which are called by my name would:

1.) Humble themselves

2.) Pray

3.) Seek My face

4.) And turn from their wicked ways

THEN WILL I

1.) Hear from Heaven

2.) Forgive their sins

3.) And heal their land

Lord, help us to humble ourselves, pray, and seek Your face. Help us to turn from our wicked ways so You can do what You do best. Thank You, Jesus!

The world could be a better place if everyone contributed one-hundred percent.

Food for thought:

Obedience is better than sacrifice.

DAY 31

REFLECTION TIME

Reading time: 9 minutes

Devotional Scripture:

"Delight thyself also in the Lord: and he shall give thee the desires of thine heart." (Psalm 37:4)

Heart To Heart:

One morning I woke up and wanted to go back to sleep and sleep all day long. Being exhausted is a feeling I had grown accustomed to due to the choices I made when I was 22 years old. Daily I now have multiple things I single-handedly must do. I got engaged to the love of my life, married, had nine children, four miscarriages, and divorced, all within the space of 22 years.

Now, my daily schedule goes a little like this: I wake four of my children up for school, get one child's clothes out, take two of them to school, take one of them to work and then go to my first job for 2 hours, then to my 2nd job. I have always enjoyed working but having two jobs is a must. I raise six of the children, feed them, clothe them, transport them to doctors, dentists, sports, friends' houses, and grocery shopping. I transport them to work and back, buy glasses, purchase shoes as their feet grow by leaps and bounds, and get their hair done or do it myself. It is next to impossible to keep up with all my daily responsibilities because they change often.

I also have a passion for helping the less fortunate, so I visit nursing homes, hospitals, the sick and those who are older and have difficulty moving about. I read Scriptures to them, pray with them, and listen to them talk. I have become a great listener. I try to hear and understand the woes and upheavals people are going through so they will not feel so alone. I receive calls from people that suffer a great deal of distress and they look to me for emotional and spiritual support. Some of them call me daily and multiple times a day. I have trouble saying no to people because I often put myself in their shoes. At times, their situations may seem unbearable or hopeless. If I were in their shoes, I would pray someone kind, compassionate, and empathetic would come to share my load or give me a shoulder to lean on. I make myself available to people because it hurts me to see people struggle. I understand I am too sympathetic. I don't really know how to stop. My dad told me I sympathize with people too much, sometimes to my detriment.

I recall one evening at church in New York. My friend had a severe asthma attack in the lady's lounge, and I extended my support to the degree that I also had a severe asthma attack. I have backed up a little. But I'm nowhere near the place I should be. Yes, I realize people take me for granted and it doesn't make me feel good, but that doesn't stop me from helping people because buried inside of me lies the love and compassion of Jesus Christ. I am living to live again. I serve others with joy most of the time. I know you are wondering why I said *most of the time*. Well, sometimes people don't take the helpful advice I give them and end up in the same or sometimes worse circumstances. The feeling that comes over me is sorrow along with disappointment that they aren't confident enough in themselves to change or make the best decisions for themselves. They don't think they are strong enough to just say no.

Dealing with women who find themselves in tough situations with the opposite sex is the most frustrating to me because women seem to be so insecure, desperate, and needy. Their occupations run the gamut, Attorneys, CEOs, Housewives, Teachers, Professors, Doctors, Nurses, and Pastors' Wives. They settle for years in relationships that are not productive and never will be. It takes an extraordinarily strong person to say I have had enough, that I love myself, and I refuse to live in this poisonous lifestyle any longer. I know through experience that no one can take such a stand without the help of God. It took me 20 years to stand up and rise to the occasion, to speak to myself in the mirror, and to acknowledge that my children and I had ENOUGH. I suffer long with people because making lifetime choices for one's future takes time. You may be in an unbearable situation as you read the words that are typed on this page. I speak directly to your psyche. Deep inside of you, lying dormant, is a reserved strength that is waiting for you to tap into it. You have the power to get out of that venomous, deadly situation.

When I began to remember how much I loved myself down through the years, it fueled me. I considered that if my mother knew what I was enduring, she would kill me. I said to myself if my dad had an inkling I suffered to this extent, and his grandchildren were in my care, he would kill somebody. Yes, I had to come to grips with the fact that I was a victim. Someone who was being verbally, mentally, physically, financially, and spiritually abused. Many years later, I found out that the ill-treatment inflicted upon me was not only the list of things I named, but my husband also went outside of our marriage and committed adultery with others. I endured inhumane treatment. I didn't realize it fully until I had a meeting with a priest that defined my situation as such. His words put things into the proper perspective for me.

Can you see yourself in my story? If so, you must rise to the occasion and understand that your safety and well-being are paramount. If you have children, you must fight for their well-being and safety as well. The resources required for your success are out there. God will put the right people in your path, and the next chapter of your life will be unfamiliar but rewarding. Freedom is a word I never cherished because I never needed to. Now I cherish it daily. You too can experience the freedom you deserve. It's been seven years now that I have depended totally on God, and I have not been disappointed. I remain thankful and full of gratitude. I love my life, and the phases of life I have experienced have been a learning process. Your future looks bright if you can find it in yourself to take the necessary steps. I encourage you today. You have what it takes to do what needs to be done. My prayers are with you. You can do it.

Food for thought:

It's alright to do something about your situation. Fight for freedom and freedom will fight for you.

DAY 32

TRUST THE PROCESS

Reading time: 11 minutes

Devotional Scripture:

"He that trusteth in his own heart is a fool: but whoso walketh wisely, he shall be delivered. Proverbs 28:26

Heart To Heart:

I remember returning home from vacation, and early the next morning, I was scheduled for chemotherapy. Oh my goodness! I had heard a lot of scary stories about others' experiences with cancer treatment. I said to God, "I will trust what You said to me in Florida." I reminded Him of His words, and guess what? He kept His promise to me. I had the first dose, second, third, fourth, and soon my doctor said, you are doing so good your body has astounded us.

He ordered testing for proof that the lump was shrinking. I took the test, and just like God said, it shrunk. It was not able to be seen microscopically. To make a long story short, I had the lumpectomy because 0.5 centimeters was left behind from a 3-centimeter lump. I began to praise and worship God! Every morning I would go in my restroom and dance before the Savior and trust the process. I will not say it was easy. But God made it bearable. I went to work every day for three months of chemo until the last one. I decided I should take the day off because they were backed up with clients, and I would have arrived too late to work.

I arrived for surgery, and they were taking so long that I told the doctor, "Let's get it on!" He laughed, and we joined hands and prayed. The anesthesiologist prayed with my daughters as well. The team took me in, and after about two hours, I was awakened to hear the doctor say, "Your surgery was successful." He said, "You will be in excruciating pain, and we will get you the meds needed for you to go home. Don't let the pain get out of control because it will be difficult to get it back under control in a timely fashion." I am not one who tolerates pain well, so I became concerned. I spent the night at the hospital because I didn't know how my body would react, and I did not want to be home without an adult. I thought I better stay at the hospital until morning because I did not want my children to see me in lots of pain. They ordered the meds and the next day the anesthesiologist came into my room to check on me. She reiterated that I would be in excruciating pain and that they were giving me enough pain meds for 24-48 hours. But after that, I needed to take the meds they were sending me home with. The Bible instructs us to be careful how we hear, so I began to plead the blood of Jesus over my body and remind God of our talk we had in Orlando.

The nurse handed me the meds and instructed me to take one tablet every 4 hours and the other one every six hours. She said,

"Please don't let the pain get out of control." I took the medicine and put it in my purse. The anesthesiologist began to engage in conversation with me concerning his family and his wife, stating that his wife had recently undergone surgery as well. He asked me to pray for her. He reached his hands out and held my hands as I sat on the side of my hospital bed. I called his wife's name out in prayer, and the anointing of God went through him, and he shook under the power of God. We hugged, and he went his way.

When I arrived home, I didn't feel any pain. The next day, no pain. The next day, no pain. It had been 72 hours and still no pain. I kept looking for the pain and began to think I had better take one of the pills just in case I fall asleep and wake up in pain. So, I took one pill. I went to sleep and woke up, and there was still not a sign of pain in sight. God took me through surgery and recovery without the expected pain. He kept His Word.

More testing was scheduled after my checkup, and new orders of radiation were ordered. I didn't want radiation. New forms of chemo were ordered at the same time. I didn't want more chemo. I wanted God to heal me, so I could be done with this horrible situation. But that was not the plan for me. Everyone has a journey, and I had to face the fact that mine was different from what I wanted.

My doctor kept reiterating that they were amazed that I didn't have side effects, that I worked the entire time. That is unheard of. I went to my primary doctor, and she said, "Your doctor is so amazed with you. I want you to know he loves you. He has sent us daily messages about your progress, and you have astonished them over there." I told her it was all God, and I gave Him the glory. She is a Christian, so we openly spoke of God's will and plan for our lives. I am now on my 13th radiation with 13 more to go and my 3rd round of chemo. I feel great because God is keeping His Word. I was off work after surgery for a month and a half. I recently went back to work on partial days, and soon (as of this writing), I'll be back to full time. God keeps His promises. The journey has not been easy, but nobody said or promised that it would be. I take life by the horns and thank God for each day. When I go into the office for treatment, they say, "here is the pretty girl!" They put music from my favorite artists on as I get treatment, and they enjoy it with me every day. The first day they asked who I wanted to listen to. I said, "I Just Want to be Happy!" and "Smile." The next day was J Moss, "Rebuild Me," Shirley Caesar, and Mali Music. Now every day, they have my music ready so when I arrive, I can zone out as I listen to the encouraging lyrics of my favorite songs.

God will make peace in the desert. Life seemed bleak, dismal, and, at points, it was as if I had lost ground. I learned many lessons during my life journey. First, it is alright to slow down. I had been going for many years non-stop. Rushing here and there and everywhere. The majority of my movement was for other people. I have always put myself last. The next lesson learned was not to pick every battle and put myself first. Originally, it was difficult to make time for Sandra, but I got over it! Now, I am able to relax and engage with what Sandra wants, desires, and must-have. Finally, I learned that knowing God is an amazing asset. Everyday, I was able to speak directly to Him and repent, refocus, re-grip, rebuild, and reconnect. Repentance is huge. The acknowledgment comes first, and then being able to tap into transparency is next. Once I began to reconnect with my creator, it was then that I felt Him taking the wheel and driving me home to my healthy lifestyle. I have no regrets; I do not have any anger for my life and the way God has orchestrated it. On the other hand, I am happy to know God was able to count on me as an example for others to know, He is faithful. My story is for His glory and for the benefit of others. It's in Him that I am able to wake up every morning with vim, vigor, and vitality. Stay tuned for the continuation of my story of "There Is Life After Cancer."

Food for thought:

I encourage you to take a deep breath and allow God the space needed to grow you. My favorite Scripture right now is, "For I know the thoughts that I think toward you, saith the LORD, thoughts of peace, and not of evil, to give you an expected end. (Jer. 29:11) Following God's plan will catapult you to your next level without enduring self sabotage.

DAY 33

PROCRASTINATION

Reading time: 2 minutes

Poem:

Procrastination is a thief,
It will rob you of your time,
The things you could have done,
And the places you could have gone.
It is NOT your friend.

Procrastination is a thief,
It will rob you of the money you could have earned,
the people you could have helped,
and the friends you could have met,
It is NOT your friend.

Procrastination is a thief,
It will rob you of your goals, dreams, desires,

and aspirations
It will rob you of your family, friends, and acquaintance
It will even rob you of yourself,
It is NOT your friend.

Procrastination is a thief 24/7,
it will steal your peace, joy, love, and contentment
it will also hinder you from
attaining heaven,
It is NOT your friend.

Written by Sandra E. Rumph-Jackson

ALLOCATION II

DAY 1

CONTINUE TO HOPE

Reading time: 2 minutes

Devotional Scripture:

"In hope of eternal life, which God, that cannot lie, promised before the world began; But hath in due times manifested his word through preaching, which is committed unto me according to the commandment of God our Saviour;" (Titus 1:2-3)

Heart To Heart:

We are born into this world and immediately severed from the sustaining nutritional flow which has maintained us through the weeks and accumulated months. Labeled full term, we are washed and bundled. But a hunger message is relayed with an expectation of satisfaction. The signals begin with a squirm, a soft nudge, smelling, searching. If appeased, a feeling of satisfaction sets in. But if not, the tears and cries begin. Without an instruction manual, instinct wakes up an inner force urging the latch on which signals the warm nutritional substance which we assume will arrive. Maybe yes and possibly no. Sometimes yes and often no. Upon each occurrence, hunger nudges a refill. We repeat the cycle. We ponder and question adequate sustenance for the hereafter. After all, a promise is a promise.

The Apostle Paul writes to his companion, Titus, assuring him that it is safe to put his hope and trust in God. He offers infallible proofs of God acting upon His Word. Just as He raised Jesus from the dead, He willingly raises believers up from the dead situations and circumstances that encompass human lives. God is committed to overseeing His creation and His thoughts are only good and prosperous, leading to a favorable conclusion.

Food for thought:

Expectation is inspirational.

DAY 2

ACKNOWLEDGE GOD

Reading time: 3 minutes

Devotional Scripture:

"In all thy ways acknowledge him, and he shall direct thy paths." (Proverbs 3:6)

Heart To Heart:

There are many uncertainties, questions, and desires to be led in a clear path. We know that it is not within the power of human beings to direct their own lives with perfect surety or that the decisions will guarantee abundance, health, and prosperity. God has given specific tools and urges us to use them whenever we need them. There is no specific time, place, or formal criteria. When we pray, it is a dialogue wherein the created speaks candidly to the Creator. A conversation with God is an exchange where one speaks while the other listens. The initiator of the conversation hails the attention, addresses the listener, speaks freely, petitions, extends thankfulness and abundant gratitude before wrapping it up. Then he or she engages in purposeful listening.

Welcomed guidance emerges, information pertaining to the previous conversation is addressed, and, very often, necessary particulars are shared. When we act upon the exchanged dialogue, the puzzle pieces of our lives fall into place exactly where they fit the best. We request, pour out our hearts, and allow the Lord to select what is best for us because He knows the proper timing and all the specifics which are necessary for us to succeed in fulfilling our earthly assignments. He never wants to cripple or handicap our progress.

King Solomon had been groomed by his father, King David. King David had forged a strong relationship with God at a young age. He became the apple of God's eye and grew up relying on God's protection and guidance. He enjoyed step-by-step conversations and God granted his petitions. Even when King David displeased God, he knew that it was safe to talk to Him. Through the acknowledgement of wrongdoing, receiving forgiveness, and changing his ways, King David walked closely with God. He was a mentor and advocate who pleased God. King Solomon observed and promised to follow and make his father's God his own. God blessed him to reign peacefully in Israel for forty years.

Food for thought:

Life is easier when God is at the helm.

DAY 3

TRUST COMPLETELY

Reading time: 2 minutes

Devotional Scripture:

"Trust in the Lord with all thine heart; and lean not unto thine own understanding." (Proverbs 3:5)

Heart To Heart:

We passionately believe in the character, strength, truth of God and place our utmost confidence in His faithful intervention to bring our desires to fruition. When we are asked to share things that we desire or cling to tightly in our hearts, we never imagine that those things are unattainable or impossible to be delivered. We look to Sages and Erudites in our communities to have words of wisdom and clarity for guidance. Yet oftentimes they are seeking God for the necessary path to navigate or the designed plan for themselves and the people who solicit their admonitions. Yet the best we can ever do is to hear and acknowledge the all-knowing Sovereign

God. It is with this fortitude that we allow our request to enter God's realm, and, without fail, we wait for the delivery.

After King Solomon had been convinced of God's faithfulness, he was able to admonish others that they had no reason to wonder what decisions to make. But they were able to rely wholeheartedly upon God moving in their favor.

Food for thought:

Favor ain't fair. But we are blessed when it hovers over us.

DAY 4

MIND YOUR OWN BUSINESS

Reading time: 3 minutes

Devotional Scripture:

"But let none of you suffer as a murderer, or as a thief, or as an evildoer, or as a busybody in other men's matters. Yet if any man suffer as a Christian, let him not be ashamed; but let him glorify God on this behalf." (1 Peter 4:15-16)

Heart To Heart:

Life is filled with happiness, sadness, fulfillment, and disappointment. Life is a series of checks and balances. The negative is neutralized by the positive. The displeasure counteracts the satisfaction and life goes on. What goes up must come down. Negative and positive are both on the same line designated by the direction of the traveler. The formula stipulates that we must suffer before reigning and pain must come before gain. We must work before we play if we intend to stay, or someone will pay. We should not kill. We better not steal. We must tend to our own affairs and stop trying to be players. Meddling in other folks' business is not the path to forgiveness. Since suffering is inevitable, why not do it with dignity and be God's witness?

While still in Babylon, the Apostle Peter exercises his authority. In his first letter, he focuses on, and admonishes about the expectations of Christianity, in addition to the duties and principles which should radiate through believers, as they suffer persecution. He insisted that the suffering should not be due to carnality, but wholly imperative as a reflection of the spirituality embedded within and synonymous to Christianity. He iterates that the scattered Jewish and Gentile Christians are a chosen people and before obtaining the promised reward, they should expect to suffer victimization as the innocent Christ had already done. Christ was their example of endurance through the sufferings.

Food for thought:

Eating the whole roll, morsels included, guarantees nutritional growth: physically, mentally, spiritually, and financially. Eat! Endure, and come out better.

DAY 5

LISTEN. GOD IS TRYING TO TELL YOU SOMETHING

Reading time: 1 minute

Devotional Scripture:

"He that hath an ear, let him hear what the Spirit saith unto the churches." (Revelation 2:29)

Heart To Heart:

We listen to the news reporter, the sports commentator, the talk show host, Momma 'nem, Big Poppa, Auntie, and Cousin Abel, but when it comes to the Word of God, why turn a deaf ear? It might not make you feel good when it ridicules the path that you follow, but if you take heed, the rewards are exponential. Clouds roll away, the sun produces a brighter day, and the rain does not come to stay. Life offers a few days filled with trouble. Therefore, endure the hard

189

knocks so that you can live your best life. Get through this, so that you can get to that.

John the Beloved disciple admonishes his audience to listen intently to the voice of the Spirit which speaks expressly to your temple housing the Holy Ghost. He is not speaking of the natural ear, which is proportioned on each side of the face due north of the jawbone. But rather, that inner receiver which even a deaf person is able to decipher. The Evangelist admonished that the possessor of the ear should apply it as a conductor of things that are good, lovely, yielding nutritious fruits of a good report. He divulges that God imparted such wisdom to him so that he could understand soon to be revealed occurrences and promises which had been signified by angelic messengers.

Food for thought:

Hear the voice. Believe the vision.

DAY 6

USE YOUR MIND, DON'T LOSE YOUR MIND

Reading time: 2 minutes

Devotional Scripture:

"Be careful for nothing; but in every thing by prayer and supplication with thanksgiving let your requests be made known unto God. And the peace of God, which passeth all understanding, shall keep your hearts and minds through Christ Jesus. Finally, brethren, whatsoever things are true, whatsoever things are honest, whatsoever things are just, whatsoever things are pure, whatsoever things are lovely, whatsoever things are of good report; if there be any virtue, and if there be any praise, think on these things." (Philippians 4:6-8)

Heart To Heart:

No one teaches us to worry. It comes natural for humans to permit our minds to feel anxiety while spending time thinking repetitively about the problematic uncertainties of probability. Fear sends shockwaves to our minds which often spark a rhythmic differential in our heart. The mind is a terrible thing to permit extensive performances of footloose and fanciful freedoms. We have been admonished to guard our minds. We are cautioned that unspoken topics of discussion, important to life's circumstances, reside in our thought recesses. Losing one's mind carries no guarantee of finding it again. It is a seriously fine-tuned engine and care must be taken to prevent a blow-out

While locked in a Roman prison, the Apostle Paul writes a short letter to the saints at Caesarea Philippi showing his gratitude for the love gift that they had sent to him. Once they heard about his incarceration, gifts followed. After which, as a parent prepares their children to fare in the world, he warns not to be deceived by other teachings or the expected actions of Christians under persecution. He mentioned people who showed exemplary characteristics for God, as well as gave the disclaimer that the Philippian brethren should rejoice through the strength that God imparted. This God-given impartation authorized accomplishments without limitation. God would protect their hearts and minds when they committed to exercising higher-order-thinking.

Food for thought:

The thoughts of your mind determine your altitude and well-being. Control that tongue!

DAY 7

THINK BEFORE YOU STEP

Reading time: 2 minutes

Devotional Scripture:

"Ponder the path of thy feet, and let all thy ways be established." (Proverbs 4:26)

Heart To Heart:

A few months after a baby is born, the inquiries begin. "Is the baby walking yet?" Sometimes it occurs early, and oftentimes late. But rarely do milestones of development fail to be recognized. Sometimes they come easy and often they are the result of training. But mechanical apparatuses are rarely engaged. Walking is the main object. Becoming mobile is the focal point. Remaining idly fixed in one place is shunned. How often do we map out our course before advancing? In anticipation, we just want to get there by any means necessary, as fast as we can, and especially before the next person. And upon arrival we pause in wonderment of what comes next. What is the expectation? What should we be doing? Where are we going? If we did it God's way, we would be sure to get God's results! He said what He meant and meant what He said.

The wise King Solomon offers thirteen delectable morsels that, if adhered to, our long lives would be full of reward, provision, and protection to be well-balanced and sensible. Peruse Proverbs 4:20-27 and grow like a spiritual giant. When we apply the necessary time to acknowledge God in all of our ways, think carefully before decisions or coming to conclusions, blessings upon blessings chase us down. It is God's will that we prosper and enjoy good health. But we must realize that the thriving of our soul is the epitome of our successful survival!

Food for thought:

Rev up the thought processes.

DAY 8

FIGHT THE GOOD FIGHT OF FAITH

Reading time: 2.5 minutes

Devotional Scripture:

"Fight the good fight of faith, lay hold on eternal life, whereunto thou art also called, and hast professed a good profession before many witnesses." (1 Timothy 6:12)

Heart To Heart:

Shadow boxing does us no good. We could lose our lives, become seriously hurt, or be incarcerated if we engage in arm-to-arm combat with lethal weaponry. Either way, the consequences are grave. When we operate in the manner that God allows, His blessing will rest upon us, flow on our pathway, and nourish the seed of our heritage. Faith is a noun which is given life when acted upon. Faith is now! Faith is the tangible part, the necessary ingredient that makes dormant things come to life. Faith is the *stuff*. Faith makes the invisible visible, the intangible touchable, and the unimaginable a reality. The evidence of faith follows closely, and hope will not allow us to be shamed. The sky is not the limit! When you reach for the sky, SOAR!

The Apostle Paul pens a letter to a young man who had a believing mother and grandmother, but whose father was not among the believers. This young man had a stomach ailment. He was younger than most of his parishioners, but these disadvantages did not count him out. Timothy was urged to fight for a successful outcome which could only be obtained as he operated in faith —making that noun into a verb because faith is, not faith was, nor faith will be. Faith is always present. The Apostle to the Gentiles admonished the young leader to obtain eternal life through the calling which was on his life. Timothy had been included in an occupation which entailed extensive training, and standardized qualifications. God had equipped him for success. He just needed to believe that he could, and then he would. Many people would witness his God-inspired achievements.

Food for thought:

Do not second-guess yourself. God called you. You did not call Him.

DAY 9

RESPOND

Reading time: 3 minutes

Devotional Scripture:

"I will call upon the Lord, who is worthy to be praised: so shall I be saved from mine enemies." (Psalm 18:3)

"Therefore will I give thanks unto thee, O Lord, among the heathen, and sing praises unto thy name." (Psalm 18:49)

Heart To Heart:

At birth we cry; the intent is to summon assistance in alleviating discomfort. As infants we cry when gas needs to be released. As toddlers we scream when we fall and skin a knee. As preschoolers we pout because someone refuses to be our friend. As school aged children we are angered when everyone moves from the lunch table. In junior high we become silent and angry because our clothes are not modern. In high school we don't know which disappointment has us crying and the people around us have no clue how to respond. Well into adulthood we operate in the fogginess of the silent cry making one bad decision after another. Finally, we meet and marry what we call our *soulmate* and - for a few years - crying becomes a thing of the past. Then we find ourselves crying again. Human responses are altogether unpredictable.

Then our yearning souls begin to hunger and thirst, seeking to be filled. This time, we cry to God. He knows and understands. Suddenly, He responds. We have made a connection and a relationship blossomed. We cry. He responds. We cry. He responds. He just wants to hear our voice. We just want to feel His presence. We need a friend. He wants to reconcile us. We say yes. He says, "Come, let us reason together." We come. We reason. He admonishes and grants desires. We live for Him who died for us. He protects us from harm. We tell people. We sing his praises. We respond. He responds.

King David, the chief musician, was elated when King Saul, his father-in-law, was no longer his enemy. God had delivered King David from this vengeful man and the rest of his enemies. He opened his mouth wide and penned these fifty verses. How will you act when God delivers you?

Food for thought:

Open your mouth and say something.

DAY 10

REFUGE

Reading time: 3 minutes

Devotional Scripture:

"God is our refuge and strength, a very present help in trouble." (Psalm 46:1)

Heart To Heart:

At birth we are not equipped to provide for ourselves. Usually, there are kindhearted people in place whose love language surrounds acts of kindness. They have been wired as caregivers for humanity. The mechanism which motivates their purpose predisposes them to thrive at a high level of performance when they are caring for, cuddling, and protecting another human. The baby knows that she is in good hands as she is assisted to the bathtub or a bandage is changed. The newborn feels the love when they are freshened up and swaddled. They feel whole although they have not yet received language, however, the signals that they emitted were validated, and adhered to. Upon awakening from a two-hour snooze an attendant is at their cheek with a fresh supply of milk, a message of care and safety is transmitted. Those hunger pains continue to come, and the delicious milk continues to be supplied. Cereal, then fruit, then juices, and then solid foods follow. The feeling of safety from the danger of hunger and neglect desists due to the welcoming, warm arms of protection. The chief musician for the sons of Korah wanted them to know that although their father had colluded with the rebels, his children need not fret or be afraid. God's strong arm of protection would shelter them and fight any enemy seeking to inflict harm upon them. God would always be present whenever they encountered trouble.

Food for thought:

In adversity God is with us.

DAY 11

MIRACLES

Reading time: 2 minutes

Devotional Scripture:

"And he did not many mighty works there because of their unbelief." (Matthew 13:58)

"Then he took the five loaves and the two fishes, and looking up to heaven, he blessed them, and brake, and gave to the disciples to set before the multitude." (Luke 9:16)

Heart To Heart:

Humanity follows the old cliché 'seeing is believing' which is not pleasing to God and is diametrically opposed to the law of the Spirit. God wants us to navigate through life using the lens of our spiritual eye. Doing so, we can observe things that have neither yet occurred nor have entered the terrestrial realm. God calls us into harmonious existence as His handiwork. As powerful as God is, we limit His ability to perform explicable events due to our suppressed and narrow thinking. When faith is operational there is no limit to the exhibits of miraculous wonders. Often, they boggle the mind, ranging from highly suspect to undeniable truths.

Embodied within the synoptic gospel passages, we are made aware of the powers of doubt, fear, and unbelief. Ask yourself the question, "Got Faith?" Faith works for the believer whether rich or poor, blind, lame, or dumb. If you can believe it, you can receive it. If you can believe it, you can achieve it and in the end you will not be forced to grieve it.

Food for thought:

God is trying to enhance our earthly existence while preparing us for an all-expense-paid trip which lasts throughout eternity.

DAY 12

SIGNS

Reading time: 4 minutes

Devotional Scripture:

"And these signs shall follow them that believe; In my name shall they cast out devils; they shall speak with new tongues; They shall take up serpents; and if they drink any deadly thing, it shall not hurt them; they shall lay hands on the sick, and they shall recover." (Mark 16:17-18)

Heart To Heart:

When making tough life decisions we often desire an indicator to assist in our search for tangible signs to convey the much-desired confirmations. Often no signs come. It is at this juncture that we inquire of God to use His powers of omniscience, omnipotence, and omnipresence to tilt the scale and guarantee a favorable outcome. We trust in the "All" which abides within the "Omni" which connects our souls to God's Spirit. After all, our souls are the breath of God. Ever wonder why it seems as though you have already been there be-

217

fore or knew that you would meet a random stranger in what turns out to not be random? Maybe you finished someone else's sentence, placing emphasis and breaks in the same places that they do. I submit to you. It is God within us!

After Christ died and rose again, he shows up at various times and people see him. In one of his last sightings, the eleven disciples were having a meal and their faith was not at the level that it should have been. They had communed with Jesus for three and a half years, observing His one-of-a-kind performances of healing the blind, the lame, and the doomed lepers. They were on the scene when He fed a meal to four and five thousand with a few fish and minimal loaves of bread. Some had seen, and others had heard about the water-to-wine phenomenon at the wedding in Cana of Galilee.

Although his followers had been gifted with insider information, they were still taken by surprise when His victimization and death occurred. Jesus reprimanded their actions, and their disbelief when the people who had reported seeing Him alive, shared what they had seen.

Realizing that they lacked the power to believe or carry out their impending assignments, Jesus instructs them to teach, preach, and baptize on a global level, launching from Jerusalem. Before he began to levitate back into heaven, He explained the signs which tag along with people who believe:

1. They would cast out devils, using His name.

2. They would take up serpents.

3. If they made a mistake and drank unhealthy or poisonous substances they would not be harmed.

4. When they lay hands, praying for the sick, they shall be healed and restored.

5. They would receive power to do greater works than what Jesus had done - after receiving the Holy Ghost.

This time they believed, obeyed, preached everywhere, and since then, God has been working miraculously through whomever he commissions.

Food for thought:

Signs follow the commissioned, when the Word is preached.

DAY 13

RECEIVE PEACE

Reading time: 2.5 minutes

Devotional Scripture:

"Peace I leave with you, my peace I give unto you: not as the world giveth, give I unto you. Let not your heart be troubled, neither let it be afraid." (John 14:27)

Heart To Heart:

Heart trouble is one of the main culprits which precipitate human demise. Therefore, John the Beloved goes right to the heart of the matter; doubt, fear, and unbelief are serious elements which chip away at our peace. God knows that humans thrive and live their best lives constantly in a state of erosion, due to the wicked one. Lucifer, the fallen star of the morning, is jealous of our ranking; one that he lost and was severed from as the outcome of rebellion which demoted him to the busybody status of trolling the airwaves. He is just not a happy camper. In his fall, he devised a plan in which he would steal,

223

kill, and destroy every earthling that he could deceive, while convincing them that he is the greatest, and that his benefit package is out of this world. He makes an offer that most people cannot refuse. It comes at a price. They do not see the deadly needle inside the juicy, bright red apple. He never advertises that the bite is laced with deadly poisons. But this is where Jesus comes in and offers life in exchange for death, peace for a troubled heart, freedom from chains, and scarlet for white. No strings attached. Already paid in full. PRICELESS! He proves to be trustworthy and reliable. He is a 24/7 bodyguard, deliverer, and provider. He handles business without negative residual effects.

Food for thought:

Do not fear, Jesus is nearby!

DAY 14

STEP ONE: BELIEVE

Reading time: 2.5 minutes

Devotional Scripture:

"But without faith it is impossible to please him: for he that cometh to God must believe that he is, and that he is a rewarder of them that diligently seek him." (Hebrews 11:6)

Heart To Heart:

In order to realize the fullness of God, who He is and what He brings to the table, we must trust His reputation and His resume. God has never failed and never will He fail. He always wins. He knows everything that is to ever be known about everything, every one, and every situation that will ever occur, including those which have already transpired. He was present before time was a thing. Before there was a when, where, who, how, or why, God was, and is, and shall always be at the same time. He is the ultimate epitome of security. He does not engage in sleeping, nor does He require slumber-time. His mind is always alert. His

227

all-seeing eyes roam here, there, and everywhere at the same time. No entity is equal to Him nor can anything compromise His power. His reach spans from before time began and will continue well after the announcement that time has ceased. What more can I say? You can trust Him! In his letter to the Hebrews, the Apostle Paul addresses the Jewish converts who were familiar with the writings found in the Old Testament canon. Because he did not clearly ascribe his name as the obvious author, anonymity shrouds authorship. It is obvious that the recipients of this Epistle were familiar even without a name attached. The practical admonitions and directives were adhered to. The superiority of Christ and His sacrificial works, practical guidelines for Christian living, and the profound emphasis of perseverance through faith were clearly set forth to these converts who hitherto did not possess the knowledge. Without faith, pleasing God was - and is - impossible.

Food for thought:

Seek God while He may be found, while He is near!

DAY 15

DOUBT NOT

Reading time: 2.5 minutes

Devotional Scripture:

"For verily I say unto you, That whosoever shall say unto this mountain, Be thou removed, and be thou cast into the sea; and shall not doubt in his heart, but shall believe that those things which he saith shall come to pass; he shall have whatsoever he saith." (Mark 11:23)

Heart To Heart:

Since we know beyond a shadow of a doubt that God created man in His own image and after his likeness, we also accept as truth that God spoke, and the entire trajectory of matter transformed. Man harbors the innate ability to speak a thing into existence, create through the power of workable imagination, and craft never-before-seen objects with the quiver of his hand wielding an inanimate object or tool. Our God is A-W-E-S-O-M-E! On His 6th day of work, God was doubly enamored

231

with His creation of man. So much so that He blew Himself inside of him and there positioned the soul of man. No other creature that was made was so fashioned, nor called friend. In his synoptic gospel, John Mark reveals that neither gender, skin color, nor dialect determined the gift to speak miracles into existence. One must believe and speak the desired outcome with no doubt in the heart. Through exercising continuous belief, the desired petition comes to pass just as it did during the days of creation in the beginning. Just make sure that you believe and do not fluctuate back and forth; then it shall surely happen for you.

Food for thought:

Lord, help thou mine unbelief. Help me to rock steady even through unprecedented times and especially as I navigate unfamiliar terrain. Let me remember to work the formula because Your faithful solution is attached.

DAY 16

R-E-S-P-E-C-T

Reading time: 3 minutes

Devotional Scripture:

"And God looked upon the children of Israel, and God had respect unto them." (Exodus 2:25)

"Yet have thou respect unto the prayer of thy servant, and to his supplication, O Lord my God, to hearken unto the cry and to the prayer, which thy servant prayeth before thee to day:" (1 Kings 8:28)

" Honour thy father and thy mother: that thy days may be long upon the land which the Lord thy God giveth thee." (Exodus 20:12)

Heart To Heart:

God's roving eyes watch over His created beings perpetually. Without faltering or pausing to rest, God deeply admires the unique abilities, individual qualities, and talented achievements of His handiwork which He has preordained to receive wisdom as downloads and timely upgrades. Daily, God loads our benefit cards even if we have not used all of yesterday's supply. Nothing is wasted. He hears our prayers even during the times when we fall short of His parental expectations. He has set us up to be fulfilled and successful as our souls prosper and are healthy. His telephone is never turned off. He receives all in-coming calls and replies at the right time. He distinguishes our voice and dialect from all other earthly inhabitants. He expects us to serve Him and only Him, listen to His voice, and follow the prompts. He offers us a long life if we respect, highly esteem, and do the right thing by our natural and spiritual parents. God chose our parents for us and determined our sibling pool. Remember that there are not many fathers!

Moses, the first leader of God's people, is referred to as the meekest man that ever lived. God entrusted Adam with power and majesty, permitting him to name the animals and his companion, Eve. They were never children. He came from the dust of the ground, and she came from his side PHENOMENALLY.

Food for thought:

Honor the parentals. Buy your house, and book your vacation. It looks like you are going to be here for a while.

DAY 17

HONOR

Reading time: 3 minutes

Devotional Scripture:

"Honour the Lord with thy substance, and with the firstfruits of all thine increase: So shall thy barns be filled with plenty, and thy presses shall burst out with new wine."
(Proverbs 3:9-10)

"And God said to Solomon, Because this was in thine heart, and thou hast not asked riches, wealth, or honour, nor the life of thine enemies, neither yet hast asked long life; but hast asked wisdom and knowledge for thyself, that thou mayest judge my people, over whom I have made thee king:" (2 Chronicles 1:11)

Heart To Heart:

God should be the first recipient of the fruit of our increase. We are blessed to be a blessing. Not everything that comes into our possession is for us to hoard as excessive collectables. When we allow God to be preeminent in every aspect of our lives, He showers us with bountiful blessings of the magnanimous kind. God has allowed it to be pressed down, shaken together, and running over. God even allows a benefactor to see you when you give God His first. No good thing will be withheld from you because you walk the walk and talk the talk. Prepare to burst through the confines that you have grown accustomed to. In essence, this increase does not fall within the level of affordability which we have attained, but due to God allowing it to become our new normal; our reality. King Solomon lost his father at a young age. The great King David earned God's respect through his repentant heart and sensitivity to God's will. Solomon carried out his father's wish, which was to build a great house for God to dwell in. God had never done that before, but He knew that this preacher/king would get the job done. Solomon did not let his father, or God down. He built that Temple! He was not selfish in his desires; therefore, God granted him blessings that he had not asked for, or even entertained. The half of his lavish accumulations has still not been told. The prestigious and renowned visited Solomon's kingdom to see whether the gossip was true or embellished. They went back to their kingdoms wowed and highly impressed! If we seek God first, God will set us up.

Food for thought:

What you make happen for others, God can make happen for you. Selfishness limits altitude and influence.

DAY 18

JOY

Reading time: 4 minutes

Devotional Scripture:

"And he leaping up stood, and walked, and entered with them into the temple, walking, and leaping, and praising God. And all the people saw him walking and praising God: And they knew that it was he which sat for alms at the Beautiful gate of the temple: and they were filled with wonder and amazement at that which had happened unto him." (Acts 3:8-10)

"Therefore with joy shall ye draw water out of the wells of salvation. And in that day shall ye say, Praise the Lord, call upon his name, declare his doings among the people, make mention that his name is exalted. Sing unto the Lord; for he hath done excellent things: this is known in all the earth." (Isaiah 12:3-5)

Heart To Heart:

Jesus Over You!

I would rather have Jesus than anything that this world is

able to shower on me. When I have Jesus, I have everything that I will ever need. Isaiah, the "eagle-eyed prophet" looked down through the line of time, some 700 years, and foretold of a Savior coming who would present as a child, a son, bearer of governmental issues on his shoulders, after being recognized, he would have many descriptive names such as Wonderful, Counsellor, Mighty God, Everlasting Father, Prince of Peace. That prophecy came true. He was born to a virgin. The angels rejoiced! He grew up in the home of a carpenter and became skilled. He is still full of wonders. He counsels the weary and is powerful in His majesty. He is our Father who will never die again. God thought it not robbery to make Him an equal. He shares His peace and tranquility with the weak and downtrodden. That repertoire is worth being happy about! We sing His praises and dance in jubilation. He reigns forever.

When He began His earthly ministry, Christ Jesus healed a lame man who had never walked before. Luke vividly describes his outward display of gratitude. Joy, dancing, leaping, singing, and praising God is normal practice for the appreciation for all He does. The Lord's reputation advances throughout the world and He is worthy to be praised. He is EXCELSIOR! No pandemic can stop Him, infect Him, or kill Him. His people should draw waters from His wellsprings using their ladle to draw upon SALVATION and DELIVERANCE from sin without condemnation or shame.

Food for thought:

When Jesus went back to the Father, he provided for any sickness that we would encounter. He took the beating for us and now we are healed, delivered, and set free by His stripes!

DAY 19

PRAISE

Reading time: 2 minutes

Devotional Scripture:

"But I will hope continually, and will yet praise thee more and more." (Psalm 71:14)

"O Lord, thou art my God; I will exalt thee, I will praise thy name; for thou hast done wonderful things; thy counsels of old are faithfulness and truth." (Isaiah 25:1)

"Let every thing that hath breath praise the Lord. Praise ye the Lord." (Psalm 150:6)

Heart To Heart:

It is good to know that the Lord is committed to being your God, the ruler of your universe, and the most reliable source of moral authority. God loves to use His power to assist with nature and our inevitable good fortune. As we leap, dance, and sing, our testimony will declare His majesty and the wonderful works He has wrought warrant acclaim and honor. We never have to search again. Once we commit, He commits. He hears our faltering whispers and faintest cries. He even knows our thoughts before we do. Anonymous psalmists concur that God is worthy to be praised with every breath that we breathe. Praise can never be classified as doing too much!

Food for thought:

We desire for God to make haste to deliver us and act upon our petitions. But what would happen if we hasted to magnify and amplify our praise for who He is and for what He has already done?

DAY 20

FAITH

Reading time: 3 minutes

Devotional Scripture:

"Now faith is the substance of things hoped for, the evidence of things not seen. For by it the elders obtained a good report. But without faith it is impossible to please him: for he that cometh to God must believe that he is, and that he is a rewarder of them that diligently seek him." (Hebrews 11:1-2, 6)

"Knowing this, that the trying of your faith worketh patience." (James 1:3)

"And Jesus said unto him, Go thy way; thy faith hath made thee whole. And immediately he received his sight, and followed Jesus in the way." (Mark 10:52)

Heart To Heart:

We must exercise our belief in the present moment. Know what you desire when you approach God in prayer. Glorify Him, identify yourself, make your request, and thank Him because you know that it pleases Him to give you good gifts, especially when they pertain to life and Godliness. The forefathers used this same formula and it worked for them. God has already made it clear that He does not operate using favoritism or nepotism. People who did not have even a mustard seed size morsel of faith obtained nothing from the Lord. Only the continuous faith walkers obtained the things that were good for them, and whatever was denied proved either to be wrong for them or the timing was not right.

When the request is delayed for an inordinate amount of time, my belief system goes on trial and the deceiver whispers sweet nothings in my ear. I fight back using the Scriptures. He runs and I obtain the victory. I must wait like Job did. God is never late. The song says that He is always on time. We just need to allow the process to unfold. Once that patience comes, we are whole, and we receive His goodness!

Food for thought:

The deliverance and the answers usually come when we least expect them. Let Go. Let God.

DAY 21

HELPER

Reading time: 2 minutes

Devotional Scripture:

"So that we may boldly say, The Lord is my helper, and I will not fear what man shall do unto me." (Hebrews 13:6)

"He brought me up also out of an horrible pit, out of the miry clay, and set my feet upon a rock, and established my goings. And he hath put a new song in my mouth, even praise unto our God: many shall see it, and fear, and shall trust in the Lord. Blessed is that man that maketh the Lord his trust, and respecteth not the proud, nor such as turn aside to lies." (Psalm 40:2-4)

Heart To Heart:

I gallantly declare that the Lord is the One who has advanced and pivoted me. He is presently anchoring me. It is not within me to set in motion the right moves while working both sides and the middle. God has the view from every angle and

255

places me in the optimal geographic region of advantage for His namesake and His glory. When God has an invisible seal of protection around me, the enemy's attempts fail. Why should I fear when faith has me anchored?

God saw me in that dark and lowly space. He rescued me, cleaned me up, set me right, and gave me strength for duty and trial because I was humble and not proud. God saw through the enemy's lies and continued to bless me over, and over, and over again. Who would not want to serve a God like this? I readily share His reputation wherever I go.

Food for thought:

My help comes from the Lord.

DAY 22

SUPPLIER

Reading time: 2 minutes

Devotional Scripture:

"But my God shall supply all your need according to his riches in glory by Christ Jesus." (Philippians 4:19)

"Now unto him that is able to do exceeding abundantly above all that we ask or think, according to the power that worketh in us," (Ephesians 3:20)

Heart To Heart:

The God of Abraham, Isaac, Jacob, and Joseph makes available the necessary elements required to bridge the gap between promise and provision. He levels the playing field by filling in every deficit until wholeness is accomplished without gaps, breaks, holes, or crevices. He uses His prosperity stored in Heaven to eradicate the entire obligation, bill, or necessity which, in times past, hampered my ability to praise Him like I should. The shackles have vanished and therefore I can dance. I hear the music above my head. He is so rich that He never needs to refill, and inventory is never depleted. When other warehouses are closed for holidays, weekends, or after hours, it does not faze God in the least. Since He is the only One that can do me like this, He is the only One that I will praise like this. Oh, oh, oh, oh I never will forget what He has done for me.

Food for thought:

His shelves are always stocked.

DAY 23

CLOSER THAN A BROTHER

Reading time: 2 minutes

Devotional Scripture:

"A man that hath friends must shew himself friendly: and there is a friend that sticketh closer than a brother." (Proverbs 18:24)

"Be strong and of a good courage, fear not, nor be afraid of them: for the Lord thy God, he it is that doth go with thee; he will not fail thee, nor forsake thee." (Deuteronomy 31:6)

Heart To Heart:

A brother always loves and is aware that he is the protector of siblings and bloodline ancestry. When danger draws near, a real brother braces himself and initiates combat. A brother is fearless and shrouds his shortcomings or selfish desires. You share the same parents or connections through unconventional circumstances. A friend networks through bonds of affection, trust, love, and respect. They never align themselves with enemies or naysayers. If necessary, they become trench buddies until a devised plan delivers both of them from harm. When they succeed, you succeed. They refuse to shine a floodlight on your shortcomings or your personal episodic woes. A friend prays before a request is evident. The connection is sanctioned relationally. Each side must remain cordial. Being "in relationship" with a friend who sticks closer than a brother, one who stands between you and the problem, sticks by you and goes before you while promising to neither fail nor forsake you is PRICELESS! Bullying is not a part of the equation. Neither is the big I little U complex. You can trust it.

Food for thought:

There is no relational divide or displaced loyalty due to His friendship with others.

DAY 24

NEWNESS

Reading time: 4 minutes

Devotional Scripture:

"And for this cause he is the mediator of the new testament, that by means of death, for the redemption of the transgressions that were under the first testament, they which are called might receive the promise of eternal inheritance." (Hebrews 9:15)

"After the same manner also he took the cup, when he had supped, saying, this cup is the new testament in my blood: this do ye, as oft as ye drink it, in remembrance of me." (1 Corinthians 11:25)

Heart To Heart:

God predestined and set-in motion the chain of events required to place Jesus in the position of arbitration.. In this position Jesus is the go-between, the mediator with skillful techniques to settle a conflict and resume peace through a series of agreements between the opposing parties. Adam and Eve fumbled in the Garden. Lucifer, the leader of the music chorale in Heaven, got beside himself. His contemporaries, Michael and Gabriel, declared war and ultimately evicted him with his large following of deceived angels. Once he and a third of the inhabitants of the angelic roster landed on earth to wreak havoc on unsuspecting humans, a negotiator skilled in prosecution and defense was necessary. Jesus willingly takes the position and God stamps his seal of approval. One of his first cases involved the body of Moses. Moses had gone up on the mountain for the last time and God informed Joshua that he was dead. Satan thought that he should claim his body, but those angels put up a mean fight. They were winning. Then Satan was winning, and nearly won. But the angels called in the One who had never lost a battle and the rest is history.

Later, as the mediator, Jesus laid down His life which satisfied God's requirement of pure blood. His blood was used as a ransom payment to justify mankind from the curse of sin and underwrite a satisfactory agreement delivering redemptive qualities in the face of the ultimate transgression. At the same time, Jesus delivers a promissory note to mankind from God, entitled "Eternal Inheritance," an agreement which in essence redeems transgressors from the Adamic sin. A groundbreaking landmark decision approved by God.

It gets better. He leaves written instructions that we should show our gratitude by washing each other's feet, drinking the blood, and eating the body as often as we can. We should remember Christ Jesus, His death and resurrection as well as mankind's induction into the classification and benefits of justification. We rise to walk in the newness of life only because of Christ's finished work on the Cross.

Food for thought:

Do not sell yourself short. You too can be brand new. Today can be your birthday!

DAY 25

COMMITMENT

Reading time: 4 minutes

Devotional Scripture:

"Commit thy way unto the Lord; trust also in him; and he shall bring it to pass." (Psalm 37:5)

"Commit thy works unto the Lord, and thy thoughts shall be established." (Proverbs 16:3)

Heart To Heart:

When humans pledge, or bind themselves, their ways, works, and their possessions to a certain course, or set of guidelines, discipline is necessary. One must not go overboard at any point. But we must remain centered and operationally positioned, focused, and ready to function within the designated parameters. You might want to make my song yours, entitled:

"Where He leads me, I will follow'

I can hear my Savior calling,
I can hear my Savior calling,
I can hear my Savior calling,
Take thy Cross and follow, follow Me.

Refrain:

Where He leads me, I will follow,
Where He leads me, I will follow,
Where He leads me, I will follow,
I'll go with Him, with Him all the way.

I'll go with Him through the waters,
I'll go with Him through the waters,
I'll go with Him through the waters,
I'll go with Him, with Him all the way.

I'll go with Him through the garden,
I'll go with Him through the garden,
I'll go with Him through the garden,
I'll go with Him, with Him all the way.

I'll go with Him to dark Calv'ry,
I'll go with Him to dark Calv'ry,
I'll go with Him to dark Calv'ry,
I'll go with Him, with Him all the way.

I'll go with Him to the judgment,
I'll go with Him to the judgment,
I'll go with Him to the judgment,
I'll go with Him, with Him all the way.

He will give me grace and glory,
He will give me grace and glory,
He will give me grace and glory,
And go with me, with me all the way.

Here is a short Scripture which is good to incorporate into your daily prayers:

"As the hart panteth after the water brooks, so panteth my soul after thee, O God. My soul thirsteth for God, for the living God: when shall I come and appear before God? My tears have been my meat day and night, while they continually say unto me, where is thy God? When I remember these things, I pour out my soul in me: for I had gone with the multitude, I went with them to the house of God, with the voice of joy and praise, with a multitude that kept holyday. Why art thou cast down, O my soul? and why art thou disquieted in me? hope thou in God: for I shall yet praise him for the help of his countenance." (Psalms 42:1-5)

Food for thought:

Jesus agrees to never leave us alone.

DAY 26

SING

Reading time: 4 minutes

Devotional Scripture:

"And at midnight Paul and Silas prayed, and sang praises unto God: and the prisoners heard them." (Acts 16:25)

"O come, let us sing unto the Lord: let us make a joyful noise to the rock of our salvation. Let us come before his presence with thanksgiving, and make a joyful noise unto him with psalms." (Psalm 95:1-2)

"I will sing unto the Lord, because he hath dealt bountifully with me." (Psalm 13: 6)

"I will sing unto the Lord as long as I live: I will sing praise to my God while I have my being." (Psalm 104:33)

Heart To Heart:

I was under the pastorate of my father, the late Episcopal Bishop Samuel I. Rumph, Sr., and down through the years he would say, "I sing from morning till night. It makes my burdens light. I am singing in my soul." I saw him in good times, under pressure, during trying times, in mourning when he buried the first and cumulative four of his children: my siblings, and when he had to bury his wife of 53 years, my dear mother, the late Elect Lady, Sister Priscilla Marie Rumph. Sometimes the voice was not as strong as it had been in prior decades, but he continued to sing. I was at his side in the vestibule of our church when he suffered a stroke. Due to receiving timely medical care many effects of the brain trauma were reversed. Through therapy he almost reclaimed everything which had been robbed during this ordeal. But he missed the pitch and control he had been accustomed to and known internationally for. Certain signature songs such as *"The Waterway"* and *"Rise Again"* were unachievable, reminders that he had been stricken in the winter of his life. Mom crossed over eighteen years ago, and Dad crossed the swelling tide seven years ago. but their songs I still remember because they never stopped singing of their own freewill. They continued to try until their final breath.

Now, I sing from morning 'till night, it makes my burden light, I am singing in my soul. I sing because I am happy. I sing when I am sad. I sing because it erupts from within my soul. I sing because I am free. I sing because I can. I sing because his eye is on the sparrow. I sing because I know he watches me. You can sing during whatever you are going through. Sometimes God will write your personal lyrics, and download them to your spirit. I challenge you to sing through adversity, as well as, in good times. I know that God's eyes are watching me. My prayer band and I often reiterate, "God, our eyes are watching you!"

Food for thought:

God is touched with the feelings of whatever you feel.

DAY 27

LOOK

Reading time: 3 minutes

Devotional Scripture:

"Looking unto Jesus the author and finisher of our faith; who for the joy that was set before him endured the cross, despising the shame, and is set down at the right hand of the throne of God. For consider him that endured such contradiction of sinners against himself, lest ye be wearied and faint in your minds." (Hebrews 12:2-3)

"Look unto me, and be ye saved, all the ends of the earth: for I am God, and there is none else." (Isaiah 45:22)

Heart To Heart:

Our eyes are windows to the soul and the pathway that lights understanding, and perpetual seeking. Words provide the imagination and stimuli to spark our journey. We listen with our ears, smell with our nose, feel through sensory receptors in our skin, taste through the buds which line our

285

tongues, and perceive through our ocular provisions. But that sixth sense referred to as extra sensory perception is the one which closely monitors our connection to God. There are also carnal, natural, and invisible apparatuses which influence our feelings and decision-making propensities that *the thing* that God gives freely to help us make decisions when we really do not know what is best? God is such a liberal giver. He does not ask us to pay for the benefits that He daily loads within us. We could not afford it even if we tried!

He made us from dirt. Yet thought to include some super with our natural, increase our abilities, and enhance our beauty through applying salvation to our souls. He wants us to behold His handiwork, His splendor, and ultimate greatness. He knows that we will become tired and faint if we try to deliver ourselves. He is the deliverer, the heavy load carrier, and the way out, over, above, and around. He wants us to depend on Him. We are not designed to deliver ourselves from what life dumps in our pathway. If we keep our eyes on God, giving thanks through praise and worship, He will handle the other particulars. He wants us to return, and thank Him because He is good. He gives everlasting mercy. He offers Himself to alleviate our shortcomings and inabilities.

Food for thought:

Can you try my Savior? What do you have to lose?

DAY 28

ASK

Reading time: 2.5 minutes

Devotional Scripture:

"Ask, and it shall be given you; seek, and ye shall find; knock, and it shall be opened unto you: For every one that asketh receiveth; and he that seeketh findeth; and to him that knocketh it shall be opened." (Matthew 7:7-8)

"If any of you lack wisdom, let him ask of God, that giveth to all men liberally, and upbraideth not; and it shall be given him. But let him ask in faith, nothing wavering. For he that wavereth is like a wave of the sea driven with the wind and tossed. For let not that man think that he shall receive any thing of the Lord. A double minded man is unstable in all his ways." (James 1:5-8)

Heart To Heart:

Ask! <u>ASK!</u>
If you **ask,** you shall **receive.**
If you **seek,** you will **find.**
If you **knock,** the door shall be **opened.**
God's Word is sure. If you work the formula, the solution presents itself.

But a man that vacillates will receive nothing. He will come close, and then roll back out, just as the waves in the water. NO —THING!

If you realize that:

1. You do not know what to do.
2. You do not know how to do it.
3. You do not know what 'it' is.
4. You are too ashamed to admit you are number 1 - 3.

Tell God all about it. Ask Him for experience, knowledge, good judgment, intelligence, and sagacity. He promises to give it to you without backhandedly reprimanding, or rebuking you. It's a win/win!

Food for thought:

The key is that all of this must be done while believing that He will do what He said He will do and that we are worth the investment.

DAY 29

WAIT

Reading time: 2.5 minutes

Devotional Scripture:

"But they that wait upon the Lord shall renew their strength; they shall mount up with wings as eagles; they shall run, and not be weary; and they shall walk, and not faint." (Isaiah 40:31)

"Wait on the Lord, and keep his way, and he shall exalt thee to inherit the land: when the wicked are cut off, thou shalt see it." (Psalm 37:34)

Heart To Heart:

The dual definitions of wait according to Google:

1.Stay put or delay action until a particular time or until something else happens. Eagerly impatient to do something, or, for something to happen.

2. To serve.

When you serve the Lord, He renews your strength. When you delay your plans, you get renewed power. When you serve the Lord and do His business, He lifts you up and benefactors know that the inheritance belongs to you. You shall receive all of the property that is willed to you. All wicked people that revolted against you shall be destroyed and you will witness their demise. They will disappear. You will not have to deal with them ever again.

When you serve the Lord, you will not miss out on receiving what is yours. You will accumulate, and gradually be increased in blessings. Your span will be large, vast, and noticeable. When an eagle is in the vicinity, everyone is aware. You are going to encounter forward progression which will not overwhelm you. You will not pass out into an unconscious state, but will have presence of mind as your blessings roll in. This will come to pass because you served in God's kingdom, and did not cheat the process. You allowed it to have its perfect work in you; therefore, soar like an eagle.

Food for thought:

You are not marking time. Actually, you are working on the BIG!

DAY 30

RECEIVE

Reading time: 3 minutes

Devotional Scripture:

"Jesus answered and said unto them, Verily I say unto you, If ye have faith, and doubt not, ye shall not only do this which is done to the fig tree, but also if ye shall say unto this mountain, Be thou removed, and be thou cast into the sea; it shall be done. And all things, whatsoever ye shall ask in prayer, believing, ye shall receive." (Matthew 21:21-22)

Heart To Heart:

"For verily I say unto you, That whosoever shall say unto this mountain, Be thou removed, and be thou cast into the sea; and shall not doubt in his heart, but shall believe that those things which he saith shall come to pass; he shall have whatsoever he saith. Therefore I say unto you, What things soever ye desire, when ye pray, believe that ye receive them, and ye shall have them." (Mark 11: 23-24)

"And whatsoever ye do, do it heartily, as to the Lord, and not unto men; Knowing that of the Lord ye shall receive the reward of the inheritance: for ye serve the Lord Christ." (Colossians 3:23-24)

"Give, and it shall be given unto you; good measure, pressed down, and shaken together, and running over, shall men give into your bosom. For with the same measure that ye mete withal it shall be measured to you again." (Luke 6:38)

Food for thought:

We know that God cannot lie and that He does not utter words for the sole purpose of hearing himself speak. We know that He is also intentional. Let us work the formula and receive our just rewards. God showers upon people who show that they are purpose-driven and focused about what they are doing, as they faithfully, and conscientiously serve Him, and His people. Eat every delectable morsel so that you may grow thereby, lacking nothing: A-Gem-A-Day!

ABOUT THE AUTHORS

From the Author

Sandra E. Jackson is the excited host of the 'Matters of the Heart with Estelle' podcast. She is a Life Insurance Agent, Facilitator, Panelist, and an Ordained Evangelist. She is currently a divorced mother of nine adorable children and has been a Hoosier for nearly five years. Sandra has a love for writing: from crafting stories to articulating poetry-she enjoys it all. In 2007, Sandra published her first bibliography dedicated to her mother entitled: 'The Greatest Mother in The World' and is now a co-author of the book 'My Hidden Strength'.

Sandra allows God to use her in several ministries, for example: hosting "There Is Life After Divorce" seminars, revivals, ministerial alliance ministry, prison ministry, and much more. On top of that, she's also an altar worker, Sunday-school Teacher, and a Soul- Winner for Christ. It does not stop there, as a woman who refuses to stop learning, Sandra is now a licensed Life Insurance Producer in multiple states. She continued her education after raising her nine children and received her bachelor's degree at Nazarene Bible College on May 29, 2021.

Favorite quotes - ***"Just Get It Done!"*** and ***"Procrastination is the Thief Of Time!" "Create A Fabulous Day", and "I Am Ecstatic To be Alive."***

Create a blessed day and do not forget to smile.

Websites: www.evgsandra.com

www.amazon.com/~/e/B08NGQ38FC

Email address: sandraspoetryspot@gmail.com

Alt. email address: greatestmotherintheworld@gmail.com

Sandra's Authors Forum:
Zoom meeting ID: 89775807782
PASSWORD: Jesus

Youtube: https://www.youtube.com/channel/UCglVU9-kfCHjgnu744MVNCg

Business Phone: (317) 565-4725

ABOUT THE AUTHORS (CONTINUED)

From the Co-Author

Pastor Beverly J. Renford was born the 7th of 15 children to the late Bishop Samuel I. & Elect Lady Priscilla M. Rumph, on August 11th, 1958, in Detroit, Michigan. At the age of five, God impressed it upon her heart, and began to call her while teaching her his voice. She was soon baptized, in Jesus' name, and at the age of eleven, received the gift of tongues.

For many years she assisted her parents in ministry. She says, "Momma and Daddy introduced me to their God, but I took it further, and now He is my God."

In June 1976, she graduated from Penfield High School. On August 22, 1981, she married Mark, and to this union eight children were born: Brooke, Bridgette, Rachel, Nicole, Benjamin, Courtney, Anastasia and Markaysia. To date, she has seven grandchildren: Shiloh and Sage, Brayden and Bryan, Preston, Penelope and Priya.

In May 2021, she graduated Summa Cum Laude from SUNY Brockport College upon earning her Masters of Science in English Degree: Creative Writing. In May of 2018, she earned her Bachelor's Degree and in June of 2015, she earned her Associate's Degree from Monroe Community College in Early Childhood Education. In 2017 and 2021 she was inducted into the National Honor Society, and the International Honor Society. She is a longstanding member of Sigma Tau Delta. In 2021, she was inducted in the prestigious Omicron Delta Kappa Honor Society. Since 2007, she has been featured in the Cambridge Who's Who, and in 2010, became the recipient of the Strathmore Who's Who. In May 2021, she was included in the 2021-2022 Marquis Who's Who in America Top Professional Book. Is a CDA member, has graduated from PLTI (Parent Leadership Training Institute), and holds licenses, credentials, and is continuously honored with awards.

In 2013, she became the Senior Pastor of the Greater Bethlehem Temple Pentecostal Church, Inc., in Rochester, New York where their mantra is "Where everything becomes Greater." This unique building is one of the Underground Railroad sites. As a teacher and preacher of the Bible, she invests in families, feeds the hungry, serves in the local soup kitchens, and is an avid presence in Clergy on Patrol; a citywide initiative which allows the residents to observe ministers and the local police, walking and talking with them, in their neighborhood.

Pastor Renford is quoted saying,"I have found that life is filled with innumerable uncertainties. Upon entry into the world, we do not know our first caretakers, our parents. After all, they have been providing care while we were in utero. We learn to trust them. Without question, we rely wholly upon their teachings while holding to their nuances, idiosyncratic characteristics, and experiences that they share. It is our parents that we become, as they decrease, and we increase. Now that we are the image, and voice in whom others aspire to emulate; therefore, we proceed without hindering or causing a crippling domino-effect? It is imperative to acknowledge God for guidance and positioning as we navigate the unchartered territories that LIFE offers."

Always remember: "It is possible to move men, through God, by prayer alone." — Hudson Taylor

Favorite quotes - *"If it is worth doing, do it right."*

Contact Information:

Email Address: bevmar8@aol.com

Business Phone: (585) 820-7816 (585) 747-3851

Authors

LEFT TO RIGHT:
Evang. Sandra E. Rumph-Jackson, and Pastor Beverly Renford

To sow into Evangelist Sandras Ministry
cash app $Sandraspoetryspot

The Rumph Family

BACK ROW LEFT TO RIGHT:
Evang. Jacqueline M. Rumph, Roderick M. Rumph, Pastor Beverly Renford,
Cherlyn E. Rumph, Eld. Lloyd, Pastor Priscilla L. Rumph,

SECOND ROW LEFT TO RIGHT:
Evang. Sandra E. Rumph-Jackson, Darryl W. Rumph, Elect Lady Priscilla
M. Rumph, Mark A. Rumph

THIRD ROW LEFT TO RIGHT:
Joanna E. Richardson, Claretta A. Rumph, Pastor Cynthia Anderson,
Bishop Samuel I. Rumph Sr., Michael J. Rumph, (Michale is holding Samuel
I. Rumph jr.), Evang. Debra D. Thomas

LEFT TO RIGHT:
Elect Lady Priscilla M. Rumph, Bishop Samuel I. Rumph Sr.

SPONSORS

I want to thank all those who sponsored this book. Please show your support and patronize them.

SANDRA'S POETRY SPOT

SANDRASPOETRYSPOT@GMAIL.COM
PHONE NUMBER (317) 565-4725

EVGSANDRA.COM

MATTERS OF THE HEART WITH ESTELLE PODCAST

SANDRASPOETRYSPOT@GMAIL.COM

PHONE NUMBER (317) 565-4725

EVGSANDRA.COM

NEED LIFE INSURANCE?

SANDRASPOETRYSPOT@GMAIL.COM
PHONE NUMBER (317) 565-4725

EVGSANDRA.COM

FOLLOW US ON
FACEBOOK

585-325-2720

GREATER BETHLEHEM TEMPLE PENTECOSTAL CHURCH

LIFE BECOMES GREATER AT FAVOR STREET
40 FAVOR STREET, ROCHESTER, NY 14608
WWW.GBTFAVOR.ORG

The Greater Bethlehem Temple Pentecostal Church extends a warm welcome to our on-site worship experience: foot stomping, hand clapping good time in the Lord. You can also join us, now... Online!!!

As Christian authors we write like our readers lives depend on it, because it does.

Are you a self-published Christian author looking to get your book on the FAITH2FAITH Online Christian Bookstore?

We are now accepting submissions. Send your request to submissions@faith2faithbooks.com

IT'S TIME TO PLACE YOUR AVON ORDER AGAIN

SANDRASPOETRYSPOT@GMAIL.COM
PHONE NUMBER (317) 565-4725

HTTPS://WWW.YOURAVON.COM/SJACKSON5720

J.W. FARMER
YOUTUBE CHANNEL
J. WENDELL FARMER

Piano Lessons $20 per half an hour
Can be reached at (317) 697-1470

Senior Associate Pastor & Head Musician
@Kingdom Apostle Ministry
Indianapolis, IN 46218

"Who is this King of glory? The Lord strong and mighty, the Lord mighty in battle. Lift up your heads, O ye gates; even lift them up, ye everlasting doors; and the King of glory shall come in. Who is this King of glory? The Lord of hosts, he is the King of glory. Selah."

(Psalm 24:8-10)